Friends of College Libraries
2nd Edition
CLIP Note #27

Compiled by

Ronelle K. H. Thompson
Augustana College
Sioux Falls, South Dakota

Ann M. Smith
Augustana College
Sioux Falls, South Dakota

College Library Information Packet Committee
College Libraries Section
Association of College and Research Libraries
A Division of the American Library Association
Chicago 1999

The paper used in this publication meets the minimum requirements of American National Standard for Information Sciences–Permanence of Paper for Printed Library Materials, ANSI Z39.48-1992. ∞

Library of Congress Cataloging-in-Publication Data
Thompson, Ronelle K. H.
      Friends of college libraries / compiled by Ronelle K. H. Thompson, Ann M. Smith. -- 2nd ed.
          p. cm. -- (CLIP note ; #27)
      Includes bibliographical references (p.   ).
      ISBN 0-8389-8002-3 (alk. paper)
      1. Academic libraries--United States. 2. Friends of the library--United States. I. Smith, Ann M. , 1960- . II. Title.
III. Series: CLIP notes ; #27.
Z675.U5T49 1999
021.7--dc21   98-49235

Printed on recycled paper.

Printed in the United States of America.

03 02 01 00 99   5 4 3 2 1

TABLE OF CONTENTS

Newsletters

Publications

Miscellaneous

CLIP Notes Committee

Lewis R. Miller, Chair
Butler University Libraries
Butler University
Indianapolis, Indiana

Roxann Bustos
Reese Library
Augusta State University
Augusta, Georgia

Jody L. Caldwell
Drew University Libraries
Drew University
Madison, New Jersey

Doralyn H. Edwards
Fondren Library
Rice University
Houston, Texas

Jamie Hastreiter
William Luther Cobb Library
Eckerd College
St. Petersburg, Florida

Jennifer Taxman
Lucy Scribner Library
Skidmore College
Saratoga Springs, New York

Mickey Zemon
Emerson College Library
Emerson College
Boston, Massachusetts

INTRODUCTION

Objective

The College Library Information Packet (CLIP) Notes publishing program, under the auspices of the College Libraries Section of the Association of College and Research Libraries, provides "college and university libraries with state-of-the-art reviews and current documentation on library practices and procedures of relevance to them" (Morein 226). This *CLIP Note* updates *CLIP Note #9*, sharing college librarians' experiences establishing and maintaining local friends groups while identifying new ideas.

Purpose

As academic institutions have struggled to find the financial resources for library support, librarians have become increasingly proactive in identifying a supporting constituency, such as a library friends group. The potential for increased financial resources is certainly appealing. Library friends programs can be viewed as a means to retain alumni interest in and support for the activities of the institution, as well as a means to develop new support groups within the community.

Background

Library friends groups have long been popular support groups for public libraries. Such groups are often the only means of funding outside a formal budget process. A core constituency of would-be supporters is readily identifiable from among a public library's users.

College libraries considering the creation of a friends group face more complex issues. Is the establishment of a separate giving "club" the best means to increase available funding? Where do you begin to identify people who might be interested in active participation in such a group? Does the college library need opportunities to generate goodwill?

The original *CLIP Note* on this topic provided a means for librarians considering the establishment of a friends group to find sample governance documents, as well as numerous examples of membership materials and event ideas. A new edition allows academic librarians to continue to share their experiences establishing and maintaining local friends groups while identifying new ideas. The compilers hope that this publication will allow new friends groups to be formed with realistic expectations based on thoughtful analysis.

Librarians working with or forming a new friends organization will certainly want to seek assistance from the Friends of Libraries U. S. A. (FOLUSA), a nonprofit organization affiliated with the American Library Association. FOLUSA's major objectives are to help new friends of libraries groups form and to encourage the development of established groups. Their newsletter, *FOLUSA News Update*, is published six times a year and is filled with news of library friends organizations and success stories.

Survey Process

The published literature on college library friends was reviewed and a survey mailed in February 1998 to 268 libraries that agreed to cooperate with *CLIP Note* publications. Recipients included those institutions defined by the Carnegie Council on Policy Studies in Higher Education as either Comprehensive Universities and Colleges I or Liberal Arts Colleges I. In addition to completing the questionnaire, libraries with friends groups were asked to supply copies of their organization's bylaws or constitution, promotional literature, newsletters, brochures, and sample programs. The returned questionnaires were tabulated using SPSS (Statistical Package for the Social Sciences) and accompanying materials evaluated for inclusion in this publication.

Analysis of Survey Results

Of the 268 surveys mailed, 196 or 74% were returned by June 1998. The survey asked participating libraries to provide institutional data from their 1997 Integrated Postsecondary Education Data System (IPEDS) report. Unfortunately, there was no IPEDS report in 1997 since those are filed in even years only, causing some confusion for respondents in providing statistical information.

Using enrollment as an indicator of approximate size of the 196 participating survey institutions, it is interesting to note that the range was 586 to 9,700 students with more than 85% of responding libraries being at institutions with enrollments of 4,000 or less. The number of librarians in participating libraries ranged from 2 to 22 with 80% having 10 or fewer librarians on staff.

Participants were asked whether they had a friends group. If the responding library had a friends group, the survey asked questions about organization, purpose, membership, events, etc. If no friends group was present, respondents were asked if they had any interest in having a friends group and, if so, what people or conditions might motivate them to begin an organization.

Libraries with Friends Groups

Of the 196 responding libraries, 46 or 24% had friends groups, with nearly one-third of those responding to the survey having been personally responsible for starting their friends organization. Of the 46 friends groups, 35 were at private college libraries and 11 were at public institutions. The enrollment range for institutions with friends groups was 586 to 6,359 (average 2,417) with from two to twenty (average 8.6) librarians on staff.

Library staff members were most frequently identified as the group responsible for having begun a college library's friends organization, with the support of the college administration and development staff. Faculty, alumni, and community members were cited as groups that were tapped for additional support in starting a college library friends' group.

Current membership of the friends groups responding ranged from less than 50 to more than 750 members. The length of time a friends organization had been in existence ranged from 1 year to 56 years with an average of 17 ½ years. It should be noted that 21 of the reporting friends groups have been formed in the past ten years.

It is of interest that of the 46 groups, 7 reported having no membership fees. The other groups gave membership fees as ranging from $1-$100 for a minimum fee to $25-$10,000 for a maximum fee.

A variety of approaches were identified as being used to recruit members, with a letter of invitation, special events, word of mouth, and library newsletter being the most popular methods, in that order. Forty-three of the groups had a librarian as a liaison; the remaining three groups, a member of the library's support staff. Time spent on friends' activities by the liaison ranged from one-half hour to ten hours each week with an average of 3 ½ hours each week. Approximately a quarter of the responding groups had a member of their college development staff assigned as a liaison to their friends group, with that development liaison spending an average of just over one hour a week on friends' activities.

Of the 46 friends groups, 36 have governing boards with 3 to 42 members and an average membership size of approximately 14 members. Board membership is determined by some form of election in two-thirds of the responding friends groups while the other boards are served by volunteers.

Activities of Friends Groups

While a few libraries report that friends' activities are planned and implemented independent of the library staff, the overwhelming majority affirmed that library staff were active in both planning and implementing friends' activities.

Clearly the most important purpose for the majority of friends groups is to raise funds for library acquisitions or special needs of the library. Other purposes cited for friends groups were awareness of library resources, events for friends and the community, advocacy for the college library, and, lastly, funds for library endowment.

Responding groups were asked how much money their organization had raised in each of the past two fiscal years. Eighteen groups or 46% reported raising $2,501-$7,000 in the past two fiscal years. In 1996-97 two groups reported raising more than $30,000, and in 1997-98 three groups raised more than $30,000. The groups were also asked for membership numbers in the same two years. In 1996-97 the membership range was 28-814 members with an average of 244.

In 1997-98, with one more group reporting, the range was 10-650 with an average of 209. There did not appear to be a strong relationship between how long a friends organization had been in existence and either the membership levels or the amount of money raised each year.

Almost all of the reporting friends groups are directly responsible for their own operating expenses, covering these expenses from any funds raised. Only a handful reported funding for operating expenses from the college development office or the library. Operating budgets ranged from $500-$6,000 with an average of approximately $1,877.

Libraries without Friends Groups

Of the 150 individuals responding to the survey for libraries without friends groups, 27 indicated that their institution had once had a friends organization which was now defunct. Where a period of existence was provided, the range was one to ten years with an average of four years.

Libraries without friends groups were asked if they had any interest in organizing a friends group for their library. The responses identified three distinct opinions regarding having a college library friends group. The first group of respondents stated that fund raising separately for their library was simply not necessary, since the administration provides adequate budget funds and the development office raises gift monies that benefit the library. A second group cited conversations with colleagues who had friends groups and/or strong impressions that the effort of organizing and maintaining a friends organization was simply not worth the benefits. In some cases they went on to suggest that they did not believe fundraising was a role that librarians should be expected to fill. The last group indicated that they were interested in beginning a friends group. Fifty-eight responded that they had not had time to organize a group to date. Several others indicated groups in the process of being organized within the year.

Respondents were asked to identify situations or circumstances that would motivate them to begin a friends group for their library. The need for additional funding for the library was identified as the primary motivator; pressure from the college administration was the second; and a staff member willing to coordinate a friends group was the third.

Conclusion

Whether respondents were from institutions that had library friends groups or not, it is apparent that the library's relationship with the college development office is a critical one. In the case of those libraries without friends organizations it is clear that, where the library enjoyed strong support from the development office and staff, there was either less motivation to consider beginning a separate library friends group or a sense that a group would be successful if the library staff were interested in moving forward.

Respondents from libraries with friends groups also commented on the relationship with the college development office. Only 13 of 45 responding indicated their organization had a direct development staff liaison. In some cases, librarians indicated that the development office was suspicious of their library friends organization believing it siphoned funds from general appeals. Again, the comments provided on the surveys demonstrated that, where the library enjoyed a positive relationship with the development office, the friends organizations were the healthiest.

It was a pleasant surprise to see how few and how mild were the frustrations cited by those working with friends groups. Many replied "none." The issues mentioned by several respondents were the challenge of working with volunteers, time commitment, low turnout for some friends' activities, and coordination with the development office.

Of the 196 participating institutions, the five libraries reporting the largest operating budgets all have friends groups. In addition, the three libraries reporting the largest materials budgets all have friends groups. The fact that the data did not demonstrate that the oldest friends groups were the most successful financially should be viewed as encouragement for any librarian contemplating starting a friends organization. With careful planning a new friends support group should be able to make a positive financial impact in a reasonable period of time.

While library friends groups continue to be found at a minority of colleges, it is apparent from the tone of the responses shared by the 46 librarians who support such organizations that those friends groups that are cultivated and nurtured provide important benefits to their college libraries. In some cases, respondents could point to such tangible benefits as increased financial support or a deliberate role their friends play as advocates to the college administration on behalf of the library. In other cases, the benefits were more broadly described as goodwill both on and off campus.

College friends groups will continue to flourish where they are embraced by the library administration, supported by the development staff, and honored by the community in which they reside. College libraries fortunate enough to have strong friends groups will find these organizations are a means to continue strengthening the resources and services they are able to provide to their constituencies.

Selection of Documents

Documents received from participating libraries represented organizational structure (constitutions and bylaws), membership brochures and promotional literature, invitations to special friends events, newsletters, bookmarks, stationery, guides to special collections or exhibits, and other publications. Examples were chosen for inclusion based on clarity of the document, reproducibility, originality of design, variety of programming ideas represented, and to provide a cross-section of responding libraries with friends groups.

SELECTED BIBLIOGRAPHY

Benefiel, Candace, LaGrange, Johanne, and Sandra da Conturbia.. "Fun, Friends, and Good P.R.: Celebrating National Library Week in an Academic Library." *C&RL News*. 53.2 (1992): 85-89.

Clark, Charlene K. "Getting Started with Annual Funds in Academic Libraries." *Journal of Library Administration*. 12.4 (1990): 73-87.

Dolnick, Sandy. "FOLUSA at 15: A Library Resource Often Untapped." *American Libraries*. 26.1 (1995): 40-42.

---, ed. *Friends of Libraries Sourcebook*. 3rd ed. Chicago: American Library Association, 1996.

Fitzsimmons, Joe. "Empowering Friends to Empower Libraries: The Future of FOLUSA." *Wilson Library Bulletin*. 69.6 (1995): 20.

Hood, Joan M. "Friends on Campus: Historical Perspective on Academic Friends." *FOLUSA News Update*. 21.5 (1998): 9.

Morein, P. Grady. "What is a CLIP Note?" *C&RL News*. 46.5 (1985): 226.

Thompson, Ronelle. *Friends of College Libraries*. CLIP Note #9. Chicago: American Library Association, 1987.

CLIP NOTES SURVEY RESULTS

FRIENDS OF COLLEGE LIBRARIES

A. General Information

Institution
Library
Name of respondent
Is the institution public or private?
196 responses: 46 public; 150 private
Number of full-time equivalent (FTE) students enrolled
196 responses: 586-9,700 range; 2,545 average
Number of full-time equivalent librarians
196 responses: 2-22 range; 7.3 average
Number of full-time equivalent library support staff
195 responses: 0-42.1 range; 10.2 average
Total materials expenditures
188 responses: $31,089-$1,642,533; $412,707 average
Total operating expenditures
192 responses: $31,196-$4,673,983; $1,075,212 average
Number of book volumes
195 responses: 15,000-1,176,930; 251,592 average

B. Friends Group Information - General

Does your library have a friends group?
196 responses: 46 yes; 150 no

C. Friends Group Information - Membership

In what year was your friends group founded?
45 responses: 1942-1997 range; over half started in last 15 years

Were you responsible for starting your college library friends group?
46 responses: 14 yes; 32 no

Rank on a scale of 1-5 those groups involved in starting a friends organization for your library:
(1 is very involved; 5 is least involved; use NA for no involvement)

College administration

very involved-------|-------------------|-----------------|----------least involved					*NA*
8	*4*	*10*	*4*	*8*	*0*

Advancement/Development staff

very involved-------|-------------------|-----------------|----------least involved					*NA*
10	*6*	*7*	*5*	*5*	*0*

Library staff

very involved-------|-------------------|-----------------|----------least involved					*NA*
26	*7*	*6*	*1*	*4*	*0*

Faculty

very involved-------|-------------------|-----------------|----------least involved					*NA*
4	*4*	*8*	*8*	*8*	*0*

Alumni

very involved-------|-------------------|-----------------|----------least involved					*NA*
5	*9*	*7*	*6*	*7*	*0*

Community members

very involved-------|-------------------|-----------------|----------least involved					*NA*
9	*7*	*4*	*2*	*7*	*0*

What is the current membership of your friends group?   *45 responses*

9	*Less than 50 members*	*10*	*251-500 members*
20	*50-250 members*	*4*	*501-750 members*

2   more than 750 members

Does your friends group have membership fees?   *46 responses*

39   Yes; membership fee range $1-$100 (minimum)
                                                      $25-$10,000 (maximum)

7   No

Indicate the approximate percentage of the total friends membership represented by each of the following groups: *42 responses*

College administrators
0% 13   *1-10%* 28   *11-25%* 0   *26-50%* 0   *51-75%* 0   *>75%* 1

Library staff
0% 11   *1-10%* 29   *11-25%* 2   *26-50%* 0   *51-75%* 0   *>75%* 0

Faculty
0% 6   *1-10%* 28   *11-25%* 5   *26-50%* 2   *51-75%* 1   *>75%* 0

Students
0% 27   *1-10%* 14   *11-25%* 0   *26-50%* 1   *51-75%* 0   *>75%* 0

Alumni
0% 4   *1-10%* 4   *11-25%* 9   *26-50%* 12   *51-75%* 5   *>75%* 8

Community members
0% 3   *1-10%* 8   *11-25%* 6   *26-50%* 11   *51-75%* 8   *>75%* 6

Others (please explain)
0% 31   *1-10%* 6   *11-25%* 4   *26-50%* 1   *51-75%* 0   *>75%* 0

How do you recruit members? (check all that apply)   *46 responses*

33   Library newsletter   *36   Word of mouth*
11   College newsletter   *37   Letter of invitation*
37   Special events   *10   Other: foundation solicitation*
                                         current board member
                                         contacts all-college appeal
                                         includes friends
                                         newspaper
                                         web posting
                                         friends are selected
                                         student membership table
                                         letters to in-kind donors
                                         friends newsletter
                                         alumni office questionnaires
                                         presentations at
                                         academic,historical,research,
                                         civic organizations

D. Friends Group Information - Governance

Does your friends group have a library staff member as its liaison? *46 responses*

   43   *Yes; library director and/or other professional librarian*
   3   *Yes; library support staff*
   Approximate number of hours/week spent on friends' activities:
   .5-10 hr/wk range; 3 ½ average

Does the college advancement/development office have a staff member assigned to your friends group?   *45 responses*

   13   *Yes*
   Approximate number of hours/week spent on friends' activities:
   .1-4.5 hr/wk range; 1.25 average

   32   *No*

Does your friends group have a governing board?   *45 responses*

   36   *Yes, if so how many members: 3-42 range; 14 average*

   9   *No*

Indicate the number of board members in each of the following categories:

College administrators
   0 *24*   1 *6*   2 *5*   3 *8*   4 *0*   5 *0*   >5 *0*

Advancement/Development staff
   0 *25*   1 *8*   2 *1*   3 *0*   4 *1*   5 *0*   >5 *0*

Library staff
   0 *7*   1 *13*   2 *8*   3 *7*   4 *1*   5 *0*   >5 *0*

Faculty
   0 *10*   1 *6*   2 *10*   3 *8*   4 *1*   5 *1*   >5 *0*

Students
   0 *32*   1 *2*   2 *2*   3 *0*   4 *0*   5 *0*   >5 *0*

Alumni
   0 *12*   1 *0*   2 *3*   3 *3*   4 *3*   5 *0*   >5 *12*

Community members

0 _9_   1 _2_   2 _4_   3 _5_   4 _3_   5 _2_   >5 _10_

Others (please explain)

0 _30_   1 _3_   2 0   3 _1_   4 _0_   5 _0_   >5 _1_

Examples: *Other university staff* *Friends of the College*
                      People who wish to use the library *Clergy*
                      Retired faculty and staff *Professionals*
                      Parents *Trustees*
                      Spouses of Administrators

How frequently does the friends board meet and for how long?   *36 responses*
    frequency of meetings: *1/yr-12/yr range; 6/yr average*
    length of meeting: *1-6 hours range; 2 hrs average*

How are the board members chosen?   *36 responses*
    4   *General election by membership from slate nominated by general membership*

    19   *General election by membership from slate nominated by committee*

    12   *Volunteers*

    1   *Appointed*

What is the length of the term for board members?   *26 responses*
    1-3 years range

E. Friends Group Information - Activities

What is the relation of your friends group to the library? (check all that apply)

    16   *Friends' activities are planned and implemented independent of the
         library*

    34   *Library staff are actively involved in planning and implementing
         friends' activities*

    5   *Other: "friends" is a special fund in development where donors can contribute,
         friends group is composed of folks who have joined primarily to use library,
         group does not involve program activities*

Rank on a scale of 1-4 the following purposes of your friends group: (1 indicates the most important purpose; 4 indicates the least important purpose)

To raise funds and/or gifts-in-kind for support of library acquisitions
Most important----------------|--------------------|-----------------*Least Important*
24   9   6   2

To raise funds and/or gifts-in-kind for support of special library needs
Most important----------------|--------------------|-----------------*Least Important*
28   5   2   5

To raise funds for the library endowment
Most important----------------|--------------------|-----------------*Least Important*
7   6   10   11

To engage in advocacy on behalf of the college library
Most important----------------|--------------------|-----------------*Least Important*
9   6   12   11

To provide special events/programs for membership
Most important----------------|--------------------|-----------------*Least Important*
15   11   8   6

To provide special events/programs for community at large
Most important----------------|--------------------|-----------------*Least Important*
10   19   6   5

To increase awareness of library as a resource for members
Most important----------------|--------------------|-----------------*Least Important*
15   6   9   12

Other (please explain)
Most important----------------|--------------------|-----------------*Least Important*
2   2   1   0

Briefly list examples of projects undertaken by your friends group in the past two years. If any of these projects were fund-raising activities, include the amount of money raised.

Fund-raising activities
     second hand bookstore on campus ($8000-10,000/yr)
     book publications
     book sales ($900, $1000, $1300, $1400, $2500, $3500, $9600/yr)
     sale of note cards
     benefit auction for the library ($167,000-215,000)
     parent's day book sale ($700-1000)

      sale of entertainment books ($1240)
      theater party ($340)
      murder mystery ($600)
      celebrity autograph auction
      annual dinner ($800)
      antiques show and sale
      art auction
      dinner in the stax
      book and paper fair ($1300)
      book fairs with local bookstore (Barnes & Noble, Waldenbooks, etc.)

Programs/Projects

      author readings, book signings, and receptions
      humanities foundation speakers
      lectures and receptions for faculty authors
      musical programs
      celebration of library anniversary
      field trips to conservation centers, press
      talks and workshops on topics such as preservation of books, papers, art works
      reading festival
      panel discussions, symposiums
      host open houses in library
      book talks
      library staff and library student appreciation functions
      banned book read-in
      created friends' homepage
      alumni librarian symposium
      Friday night poetry readings with regional poets
      children's story hour
      exhibits: art, photography, handmade books

Projects funded

      purchase of special collections (letters, $10,000)
      scholarship for graduating senior ($800/yr)
      ongoing purchase of books for special collections
      digitization of college archives
      provide prizes for essays during National Library Week
      provide prizes for a WWW scavenger hunt to promote library homepage
      purchase of microfilm reader printer
      establishment of endowment
      purchase of books in honor of graduating library student assistants
      library computerization
      browsing (recreational reading) collection
      purchase of library furniture
      acquisition of manuscript collections

(Projects funded continued)

　　　sponsorship of summer internship program for student interested in librarianship
　　　conservation of materials

How much money was raised, including gifts-in-kind, by your friends group in each of the past two fiscal years? Please indicate membership in each year.

1996-97 *(38 responses)*	6	$ 0-2,500
	18	$ 2,501-7,500
	8	$ 7,501-15,000
	5	$15,001-30,000
	2	*if over $30,001, how much?*
		$38,493, $43,219

Membership: 28-814 range; 244 average

1997-98 *(39 responses)*	7	$ 0-2,500
	18	$ 2,501-7,500
	6	$ 7,501-15,000
	5	$15,001-30,000
	3	*if over $30,001, how much?*
		$40,381, $41,533, $240,000

Membership: 10-650 range; 209 average

What is the amount and source of funds for the current operating budget (postage, copying, etc.) of your friends group? *20 responses*

Amount: $500-$6,000 range; $1,877 average

Source: 42 responses

3	*College funds through Advancement/Development office*
3	*College funds through Library*
35	*Friends raise all funds for operating expenses*
1	*Other*

Please list the three most important benefits for your library as a result of having a friends group: *(number in parentheses indicates frequency of response)*

> *direct financial support for library collections, services, programs (27)*
> *community awareness and support of library (18)*
> *good publicity and visibility (16)*
> *funding for special library projects (10)*
> *programs that bring people to library/campus (7)*
> *positive link to alumni and current students (7)*
> *campus support/visibility (5)*
> *encouragement of other gifts to library (4)*
> *establish endowment and planned giving awareness (4)*
> *strengthens special collections (3)*
> *members enjoy programs and borrowing privileges (2)*
> *sponsoring authors on campus (1)*
> *involves community in life of college, community outreach (1)*
> *encourage faculty support for and understanding of library (1)*
> *built tons of goodwill (1)*
> *advocate to college Board of Trustees on behalf of the library (1)*
> *source of volunteers for library (1)*
> *effective way to extend circulation privileges to non-institution patrons (1)*
> *group provides evidence of community support when seeking grant funding*
>   *for any library project (1)*

Please indicate any issues created by having a friends group that result in frustration:

> *challenge of working with volunteers who may not always follow through*
> *time commitment on part of library director and other members of library staff*
> *friends compete with students for use of library space and resources*
> *low attendance at some special events*
> *coordination with other development activities on campus, selection of mailing*
>   *dates for membership appeals*
> *lack of formal organization for group*
> *volunteers may be reluctant to undertake fund raising activities*
> *lack of support from administration, development, faculty*
> *challenge of increasing membership*
> *focusing attention of friends on issues identified as critical by library staff*

Would you start a friends group for your college library if you did not already have one? *(42 responses)*

39   *Yes*

3   *No; if no, why?*

Reasons: *Commitment of time*
                  Other priorities
                  Insufficient staff for workload

Would your Advancement/Development Office encourage you to start a friends group if you did not already have one?   *(139 responses)*

76   *Yes*

63   *No; if no, why?*

Reasons: *Lack of understanding of what a friends group can and is doing*
                  Concern that friends groups divert funds from annual campaign
                  Insufficient staff to support
                  Viewed as competitor in fund raising
                  Overlap with other fund raising appeals
                  Too much work for monetary return
                  Interest in keeping "giving clubs" to a minimum

F. Libraries Without Friends Groups

We had a friends group but it is now defunct. *27*
        If so, how long did it exist? *1-10 years range*
What reasons contributed to this?
        lack of support, interest, time
        difficulty recruiting members
        combined with other giving clubs to form a single appeal
        administrative decision (president, development officer) to discontinue

Rank on a scale of 1-5 the following reasons why your library does not have a friends group
        (1 is most important reason; 5 is least important reason; NA for not applicable)

We are interested but have not had time to organize such a group

Most Important-----|-----------|----------|------*Least Important*					*Indicated/not ranked*	*NA*
42	*16*	*10*	*12*	*12*	*6*	*14*

No interest on part of library staff in organizing

Most Important-----|-----------|----------|------*Least Important*					*Indicated/not ranked*	*NA*
21	*32*	*19*	*10*	*14*	*4*	*17*

No support from alumni/community members in organizing

Most Important-----|-----------|----------|------*Least Important*					*Indicated/not ranked*	*NA*
6	*15*	*29*	*20*	*17*	*3*	*16*

No interest on part of college administration in organizing

Most Important-----|-----------|----------|------*Least Important*					*Indicated/not ranked*	*NA*
27	*31*	*20*	*13*	*12*	*7*	*12*

Public library in community already has a strong friends organization

Most Important-----|-----------|----------|------*Least Important*					*Indicated/not ranked*	*NA*
8	*6*	*10*	*9*	*30*	*1*	*31*

Other (please explain)

Most Important-----|-----------|----------|------*Least Important*					*Indicated/not ranked*	*NA*
16	*3*	*2*	*1*	*0*	*7*	*9*

    Reasons: *Perception that the time and energy required to support friends groups*
        far exceed the value received.
        Staff is small with little time to do the work
        Do not want to "compete" with other college development efforts
        Located in small town, believed to lack sufficient base
        All income goes to university's general fund, therefore no potential for
        additional income to library
        No need
        Other academic institution in town has strong friends organization

Rank 1-5 the following as to their effectiveness in motivating you to begin a friends group for your college library: (1 is most important reason; 5 is least important reason)

Pressure from administration

Most Important-----|-----------|----------|------Least Important					Indicated/not ranked	NA
31	19	8	21	12	3	0

Need for additional funds for library

Most Important-----|-----------|----------|------Least Important					Indicated/not ranked	NA
39	16	24	10	2	2	0

Source of ideas/support for friends programming

Most Important-----|-----------|----------|------Least Important					Indicated/not ranked	NA
3	21	30	29	6	0	0

Willing library staff member to volunteer to serve as coordinator

Most Important-----|-----------|----------|------Least Important					Indicated/not ranked	NA
24	32	20	6	9	1	0

Other (please explain)

Most Important-----|-----------|----------|------Least Important					Indicated/not ranked	NA
4	2	1	1	7	1	4

Reason: *Promote library services to the community*
If lack of friends perceived as critical weakness of library
To raise funds for specific purposes, i.e. new building, special collections
Good outreach into community as well as fund raising
Clear mission to support library's primary purpose
Need for community outreach
Belief that friends group would be best way to raise additional funding

DOCUMENTS

Constitutions & Bylaws

Membership Brochures

Program Ideas

Newsletters

Publications

Miscellaneous

Constitutions and By-laws

Mabee Library
Washburn University
1700 College
Topeka, KS 66621

Library
Southern Oregon State College
1250 Siskiyou Blvd.
Ashland, OR 97520-5076

Jessie Ball DuPont Library
University of the South
Sewanee, TN 37375-1000

Library
Evergreen State College
Olympia, WA 98505

FRIENDS OF MABEE LIBRARY
Washburn University
BYLAWS

Section 1 - Purpose of Organization

Mission Statement. The Friends of Mabee Library at Washburn University shall encourage, organize and seek support for the library, to enrich the cultural and intellectual climate of the area through its general and special collections

Section 2 - Office

Principal Office. The principal office for the transaction of the business of the organization is located at Washburn Endowment Association, Topeka, Kansas.

Section 3 - Membership

Members. All those who contribute to the Friends of Mabee Library at Washburn Univesity shall be considered members of the group.

Place of Meetings. All membership meetings shall be held at such times and places as may be designated by the Board of Trustees.

Section 4 - Trustees

Board of Trustees. The general affairs of the organization shall be managed by a board of five (5) to eleven (11) trustees who are elected by the membership at each annual meeting of membership (or a special meeting if a vacancy on the board of trustees is not filled at an annual meeting). The Director of Mabee Library shall be a member of the Board of Trustees and shall act as Chair of the Trustees until the president is elected. The board of trustees shall have the following powers including those specifying that certain actions must be authorized or approved by the membership:

First - To elect and remove the officers, agents and employees of the organization, prescribe their powers and duties, fix their compensation, and may require from time to time security for faithful service.

Second - To control the affairs and business of the organization.

Third - To appoint an executive committee, composed of at least three trustees, and to delegate to such executive committee any of the powers and authority of the board of trustees in the management of the affairs of the organization between the times of regular meetings of the board of trustees.

Term of Office. Approximately one-third of the first trustees shall be elected for terms of one, two, and three years, respectively. Thereafter, trustees shall be elected so that the terms of office will expire each year for approximately one-third of the incumbent trustees. Except for the initial one and two year terms given the orginal trustees, the term for any trustee shall be three years.

Removal of Trustees. Trustees shall hold office until their respective successors are elected. A trustee may be removed from office only upon written notification from the membership, who may exercise such power of removal without cause.

Vacancies. Vacancies on the board of trustees may be filled by election by remaining trustees until the next annual meeting of the membership.

Fees and Compensation. Trustees shall not receive any compensation for their services as trustees, but, by resolution of the board of trustees, may be reimbursed for reasonable expenses paid or incurred in attending meetings of the board of trustees or a committee of the board or in performing other services for the organization.

Section 5 - Officers

Officers. The officers of the organization shall be a president, vice president, a secretary, and a treasurer.

Election. The officers of the organization shall be chosen annually by the board of trustees, and each shall hold office until he or she shall resign, be removed or disqualified to serve, or until a successor shall be appointed or elected.

Subordinate Officers. Etc. The board of trustees may at any time appoint other officers and specify their duties, authority, tenure as the business of the organization may require.

Removal. An officer may be removed without cause by the board of trustees.

President. A member of the board of trustees shall be elected president of the organization. The president shall be chief officer of the organization, chair of the board of trustees, and shall preside at all meetings of the trustees.

Vice President. A member of the board of trustees shall be elected vice president of the organization. The vice president shall serve in the absence or disability of the president, and perform the duties and exercise the authority of the president. The vice president shall also be vice chair of the board of trustees and shall have such other powers and duties as may be prescribed by the board of trustees.

Secretary. A member of the board of trustees shall be elected secretary of the organization. The secretary shall keep minutes of all meetings of the board of trustees and membership, shall maintain a membership ledger, shall give notice of meetings of the membership and of the board of trustees as required by these bylaws, and shall have such other powers and perform such others duties as may be prescribed by the board of trustees or these bylaws.

Treasurer. A member of the board of trustees shall be elected treasurer. The treasurer shall monitor accounts of the properties and business transactions of the organization which shall at all reasonable times be open to inspection by any trustee. These accounts shall be maintained by the Washburn Endowment Association and managed by the office of the Director of Mabee Library.

Section 6 - Meetings

Annual Meeting. The membership shall meeting [sic.] during the month of June to elect trustees and to transact other business properly brought before the meeting.

Special Meetings of Membership. The membership may call a special meeting at any time. A special meeting shall be held between the hours of 9 o'clock a.m. and 9 o'clock p.m. on any day of the week, at a place specified by the person(s) calling the meeting.

Notice of Membership Meetings. Notice of an annual meeting shall be mailed to each member, at his or her address shown on the organizations records, not less than seven (7) nor more than thirty (30) days preceding the day of the meeting. Notice of a special meeting of the membership shall be given to each member not less than seven (7) days before the day of the meeting. Any notice shall state the time, date, place, and purpose of the meeting. At meetings of membership, the members present shall constitute a quorum.

Meeting of the Board of Trustees

(a) Initial meetings. The initial meeting of the trustees shall be held at the place of and immediately following adjournment of the annual membership meeting, to elect officers and to transact other necessary business.

(b) Regular meetings The board of trustees shall, by resolution, fix the time, dates, and place of its regular meetings and shall give notice to each trustee at least one (1) day before the day of each meeting; but if a trustee cannot conveniently be reached personally or by telephone no notice of the meeting need to be given.

(c) <u>Special meetings.</u>   The board of trustees shall meet specially at the call of the President, or four (4) or more trustees. Notice of the time, place and purpose of a special meeting shall be given to each trustee at least one (1) day before the day of the meeting.

Waiver of Notice.   Notice of any meeting of the membership or the board of trustees may be waived by a writing signed by the person so waiving and delivered to the secretary. A person who attends a meeting without making objection to the failure to give proper notice of the meeting shall be deemed to have waived such notice.

Written Consent.   The trustees may consent to an action in lieu of a meeting.

Quorum.   A majority of the trustees must be present at a meeting of the board of trustees in order to transact business. However, those present at a meeting of the board of trustees, although less than a quorum, may adjourn the meeting to the same place and hour on a subsequent business day within ten (10) days thereafter without further notice. If a quorum is not present at the adjourned session, then a new notice of the meeting must be given to all trustees.

Voting.   Each trustee shall have one vote on any matter submitted to the board of trustees. The vote of a majority of the trustees who are present at a meeting shall be the act of the board of trustees unless a different vote is required by law or these bylaws.

Section 7 - Miscellaneous

Liability of Trustees.   A trustee shall not be liable to the organization or its membership for monetary damages for breach of fiduciary duty as a trustee, subject to the exceptions set in K.S.A.Section 17-6002(b) (8) as the same now exists or as it may be amended hereafter.

Checks, Drafts. Etc.   All checks, drafts or other orders for payment of money, notes or other evidences of indebtedness, issued in the name of or payable to the organization, shall be signed or endorsed by such person or persons and in such manner as, from time to time, shall be determined by resolution of the board of trustees, the Washburn Endowment Association and Mabee Library Director.

Contracts, Deeds, Etc., How Executed.   The board of trustees, except as in these bylaws or otherwise provided, may authorize any officer or officers, agent or agents, to enter into any contract or execute any instrument in the name of and on behalf of the organization, and such authority must be confined to specific instances; and unless so authorized by the board of trustees, no officer, agent or employee shall have any power or authority to bind the organization by any contract or engagement or to pledge its credit or to render it liable for any purpose in any amount; provided, however, that any contracts, agreements, deeds or other instruments conveying land or any interest herein, and any other documents shall be executed on behalf of the organization by agreement of the membership.

Fiscal Year. The fiscal year of the organization shall commence on July 1 and end on June 30 of each year.

Section 8 - Amendments

Power of Trustee. New bylaws may be adopted or these bylaws may be amended or repealed by a majority vote of the board of trustees at any regular or special meeting thereof; provided, however, that the time and place fixed by the bylaws of the annual election of trustees shall not be changed within sixty (60) days next preceding the date on which such elections are to be held. Notice of any proposed amendment of the bylaws by the board of trustees shall be given to the membership at least twenty-one (21) days prior to the date such proposed amendments will be voted on by the board. Any new or amended bylaws must be approved in writing by the membership prior to adoption by the Board.

ADOPTED THIS _____ day of _____ . 1996

CONSTITUTION
FRIENDS OF THE LIBRARY
SOUTHERN OREGON STATE COLLEGE

ARTICLE I

Name. The name of the organization shall be the Friends of the Library at Southern Oregon State College.

ARTICLE II

Purpose. The purpose of this organization shall be three-fold: to foster beneficial relations between the Southern Oregon State College Library and the residents of the region it serves; to assist in the growth and development of the Library's resources and services, with particular respect to its special collections; and to provide for all interested persons an active forum for the interchange of information about books and book collecting.

ARTICLE III

Membership. Members of the Friends of the Library at the time of adoption of this constitution and others hereafter joining shall constitute the membership.

ARTICLE IV

Limitations. No part of the net income of the Friends, from membership dues or other sources, shall serve the particular benefit of any member; all funds shall be used for the benefit of the Southern Oregon State College Library.

ARTICLE V

Government. The government of the Friends shall be vested in a Board of Directors of not fewer than five members nor more than nine members, who shall be elected for two-year terms. Half of the Board members shall be elected each year. In addition, the Board of Directors shall include as ex-officio and non-voting members the President of Southern Oregon State College or his/her designee, a representative designated by the Southern Oregon State College Foundation, and the Library Director. No more than two voting positions on the Board shall be occupied at any one time by members of the faculty or administration of Southern Oregon State College. No Board member shall serve more than three consecutive terms.

The Board of Directors shall have the power to make and to amend by-laws consistent with the provisions of this constitution, but only with the approval of two-thirds of the members present and voting at a regular meeting.

The Constitution may be amended only at the annual spring meeting by a two-thirds vote of the membership present, after the membership has been notified by mail thirty days prior to the meeting.

Revised and approved May 9, 1987.

BY-LAWS
FRIENDS OF THE LIBRARY
SOUTHERN OREGON STATE COLLEGE

ARTICLE I
Membership

Section 1. Any person, business firm, or corporate body interested in the purposes of the Friends may become a member by payment of the appropriate membership fee.

Section 2. The Board of Directors shall *fix* and from time to time review the amounts of the membership dues. Membership categories shall be:

- Life Members
- Sustaining Members
- Business and Institutional Members
- Contributing Members
- Regular Members
- Student Members
- Senior Citizen Members

Section 3. The membership year shall be from June 1 of the current year through May 31 of the following year.

Section 4, Honorary membership may be awarded by a vote of the Board of Directors to individuals or organizations who make notable contribution to the Library or the Friends.

ARTICLE II
Board of Directors

Section 1. A vacancy on the Board of Directors shall be filled by a vote of the remaining Board members, effective until the next annual election when a new Board member shall be elected for the remainder of the term.

Section 2. A majority of the members of the Board shall constitute a quorum for the transaction of business.

Section 3. All actions of the Board shall be by a majority vote of those present and voting.

Section 4. Regular meetings of the Board shall be held at times and places specified by the Board; special meetings shall be called as appropriate with due notice to all Board members.

Section 5. The Board may appoint standing committees and committees for special purposes.

Section 6. Board members shall be elected by members present at the Annual Spring Meeting. Board members shall hold office from the end of that meeting to the end of the meeting two years later.

ARTICLE III
Officers

Section 1. The officers of the Friends of the Library shall be a president and vice-president; they shall be elected annually by the Board of Directors at its first meeting after the Annual Spring Meeting. A Secretary shall be appointed by the Board at the same time.

Section 2. The Board shall have the power to fill vacancies in the above offices.

Section 3. The duties of the respective officers shall be:

President: To preside at meetings; be responsible for arranging speakers and other activities at meetings and any special programs, with the assistance of the vice-president and secretary.

Vice-President: To preside in the absence of the president; be responsible for maintaining the membership roster and serve as membership chair; assist the president with programs and meetings.

Secretary: To record and preserve the minutes of the Board meetings and the business meetings of the general membership; be responsible for mailing meeting announcements and other information to members; assist the president with programs and meetings.

ARTICLE IV
Finances

Section 1. All money received from whatever source shall be deposited with the Southern Oregon State College Foundation in accounts in the name of the Friends of the Library.

Section 2. The fiscal year of the Friends shall be that of the Southern Oregon State College Foundation.

Section 3. Expenditures from the above accounts shall be made by the Library Director under the authorization of the Board of Directors.

Section 4. A report of receipts and expenditures shall be made to the general membership at the annual spring meeting.

ARTICLE V
Dissolution

Section 1. In the event of dissolution of the Friends of the Library organization, all residual assets shall be transferred to an appropriate agency for continuance of the purposes stated in the Constitution of the Friends.

Revised and approved October 9, 1995.

CONSTITUTION OF THE
FRIENDS OF THE LIBRARY
OF THE UNIVERSITY OF THE SOUTH

ARTICLE I --NAME

The name of this organization shall be Friends of the Library of the University of the South.

ARTICLE II -- PURPOSES

The purposes of the organization shall be:

To stimulate interest in the collections and facilities of the library of the University of the South.

To provide opportunity for those interested in the library to participate in exhibits, programs, and publications.

To attract gifts of books, manuscripts, and other materials for the enrichment of the resources of the library.

ARTICLE III -- MEMBERSHIP

Membership will be open to any person or organization subscribing to these purposes. Classes of membership and dues shall be determined by the Governing Board.

ARTICLE IV -- GOVERNING BOARD & OFFICERS

There shall be a Governing Board composed of six voting members, elected by the membership at two per year for three year terms, plus the University Librarian who shall have vote only to resolve a tie.

In addition to the elected Governing Board, the membership may elect Honorary Members of the Governing Board, but these shall have no vote.

All members, including Honorary Members shall be eligible for regular election to the Governing Board.

The Governing Board shall meet annually to elect, for one year terms or until their successors shall be elected, a President, a Vice President, and a Secretary-Treasurer.

Additional meetings may be called as necessary.

The Governing Board shall deal also with such matters and plans as shall advance the stated purposes of the Friends of the Library, forwarding appropriate resolutions to the stated meetings, and coordinating its work with the operation of the Library.

The Governing Board shall prepare and adopt, and amend as necessary, by-laws for the conduct of their affairs.

ARTICLE V -- MEETINGS

A general annual meeting shall be held.

As need arises, on 20 days' notice, special meetings of the membership may be called either by the Governing Board or by petition of any 20 members. In every such case, the purpose of the meeting must be stated.

The Governing Board shall be responsible for arranging the meetings and for notifying the whole membership of the time and place they will be held.

ARTICLE VI -- AMENDMENT

This constitution may be amended by a vote of two-thirds of the members present at any general annual meeting or at any special meeting called for that purpose.

Adopted at the annual general meeting on April 20, 1991.

BY-LAWS
OF
FRIENDS OF THE EVERGREEN STATE COLLEGE LIBRARY
****

I.
NAME

The name of this corporation shall be and hereby is declared to be **FRIENDS OF THE EVERGREEN STATE COLLEGE LIBRARY**, a NONPROFIT MUTUAL CORPORATION.

II.
DURATION

The period of its duration is perpetual.

III.
PURPOSES

The object and purposes for which this corporation is formed and the powers which it shall have and exercise are hereby agreed and declared to be as follows:

1. To further understanding, acceptance and support of the values of The Evergreen State College by the public through the visibility and services of the institution's library.

2. To support the work of The Evergreen State College Library and to provide an understanding of the importance of its work to the college and to the public community.

3. To assist members of the public to become better acquainted with The Evergreen State College through its library. To support improvement of the Evergreen Library and to link its resources with the needs of the college community, alumni, and members of the public.

4. To engage in all activities necessary or proper for the advancement and promotion of the general objectives set forth above.

5. To solicit, receive and accept donations of money or property in kind to be used solely for the advancement of the general objectives of this corporation as set forth above.

6. To assume and exercise all rights, powers and privileges that are now or hereafter may be conferred by law upon nonprofit mutual corporations, and specifically

including those powers enumerated by Section 24.06.030 of the Revised Code of Washington.

7.   Notwithstanding any other provision of these Articles, this corporation shall not carry on any activities not permitted to be carried on by an organization exempt from Federal Income Tax under Section 501(c) (3) of the Internal Revenue Code.

IV.
BOARD OF DIRECTORS

The Board of Directors shall manage the affairs of this corporation. The number of the directors shall be not less than 5 nor more than 30. One third of the directors to be elected at the first membership meeting shall be elected for a term of one year, one third of said directors shall be elected for a term of two years, and one third of said directors shall be elected for a term of three years. Thereafter at each annual meeting directors shall be elected for a term of three years to succeed the directors whose term shall expire at the time of such meeting. All directors so elected shall hold office for the term of which they are elected and until their successors are elected and qualified. Board of Directors should be members of the corporation for at least one year prior to election.

The Board of Directors shall meet every 4 months, or more as needed. Written notice of the time and place of the meeting with a proposed agenda will be sent to each Officer and Board of Directors member.

The Board of Directors positions shall be filled by those candidates receiving the highest number of votes except at least 2 members of the Board shall be designated by the Alumni Association Board of Directors and at least 2 directors shall be members of the faculty.

V.
EX-OFFICIO DIRECTORS

The Dean of the Evergreen Library shall serve as an Ex-Officio member of the Board with vote and voice. The Executive Director of The Evergreen College Foundation, the College President, the Director of College Relations and the recording secretary shall also serve as Ex-Officio members of the Board with vote and voice.

VI.
MEMBERSHIP

Membership in this corporation will be open to all individuals in sympathy with its purposes. Each individual member will be entitled to one vote. Annual membership dues will be:

Student/Senior	$ 5.00
Individual	$ 5.00
Contributor	$ 25.00
Household	$40.00
Supporting Member	$ 60.00
Sustaining Member	$100.00
Patron	$250.00
Benefactor	$500.00
President's Club	$1,000.00 or more

The membership year shall be the calendar year. In January each year the Membership Committee shall conduct an annual membership drive.

VII.
OFFICERS

The officers of this corporation shall be a president, vice-president, secretary and treasurer. Officers shall be nominated by a nomination committee chosen by the Board of Directors, which shall submit nominations in writing to the Board of Directors two weeks prior to the annual meeting. Officers should be members of the Friends of the Evergreen State College Library for one year or more prior to election. Additional nominations may be made from the floor at the annual meeting with the consent of the nominee. Voting for officers will be by written ballot of those members present at the annual meeting. Officers should be members of The Evergreen State College Library for one year or more prior to election.

Officers shall be elected by plurality vote of those members who are in good standing as members of the corporation and who are present at the annual meeting. The term for officers shall be for two years, or until their successors have been elected and qualified, and shall begin immediately following the annual meeting. Officers may be re-elected.

The vice-president will automatically assume the office of president after the president's term has expired, or at any time should the office of president be vacated. Other vacancies among offices may be filled by Board of Directors' appointment and such officers so appointed shall hold office until their successors have been elected and qualified at the next annual membership meeting.

VIII.
DUTIES OF OFFICERS

The officers of this corporation shall have the usual duties and authority exercised by officers of a nonprofit mutual corporation. The president shall be an ex-officio member of all committees. The vice-president shall serve as president in the absence of the president. The Treasurer shall render regular financial reports. In addition, the President shall appoint an Auditing Committee at least one month prior to the annual meeting. The Auditing Committee will submit a written report to the membership at the annual meeting.

IX.
EXECUTIVE BOARD

The Executive Board shall consist of the elected officers of the organization, and the Dean of the Library ex-officio. The Executive Board shall have the authority to appoint committees, collect membership dues, and conduct all business consistent with the purposes of this organization and to exercise all powers of the Board of Directors. Meetings of the Executive Board shall be held as needed. A simple majority of the Executive Board shall constitute a quorum.

X.
MEMBERSHIP MEETINGS

Meeting of the membership of this corporation shall be held at least once a year. The annual meeting will be held on a day in the fall quarter of each year, to be determined by the Executive Board.

I.   Regular membership meetings shall be at The Evergreen State College. The location may be changed by a majority of the Executive Board or the Ex-officio Executive with the approval of the President.

II.   The Annual Meeting shall be the regular meeting in Fall quarter of each year and shall be at The Evergreen State College Library.

III.   Special Meetings. The President, or any 5 members of the Board or 5% of the membership, may call a special meeting of the membership.

IV.   All meetings shall be announced by written notice at least 14 days before the meeting. Special meeting notices will contain a statement of the purpose of the meeting and the names of the people requesting the meeting.

V.   A quorum for general and special meetings shall consist of those members present.

VI.   Voting on all matters <u>EXCEPT</u> election of officers and board members shall be by voice vote unless otherwise called for by a majority of members present. A simple majority of those present and voting shall approve or disapprove all motions.

XI.
MISCELLANEOUS PROVISIONS

This corporation is not organized for the purpose of carrying on any business, trade, vocation or profession for profit, and to that end: (a) no part of the income or assets of this corporation shall at any time inure directly or indirectly to the benefit of any individual, member, officer, or director, or be distributable to any such person by any means whatsoever. Upon dissolution or final liquidation of this corporation, the assets of this corporation shall be applied first to the discharge or satisfaction of all outstanding obligations and liabilities of the corporation and remaining assets of the corporation after payment of such obligations and liabilities shall be distributed to The Evergreen State College Foundation, which has established its tax-exempt status under Section 501(c) (3) of the Internal Revenue Code; (b) this corporation shall not at any time make any loans to any of its officers, directors, employees or members of the corporation. Any member of the directors who votes for or consents to the making of a loan to any such person or any officer who participates in the making of such loans shall be jointly and severally liable to the corporation for the full amount of any such loan until the repayment thereof.

XII.
AMENDMENTS

Amendments to the By-laws of this corporation may be made by the Board of Directors: provided, that no Executive Board of the Board of Directors shall have the authority of the Board of Directors in reference to amending, altering or repealing the by-laws.

Revised: March 9,1998

Membership Brochures

Murray Learning Resources Center
Messiah College
Grantham, PA 17027-9990

Oberlin College Library
Oberlin College
Oberlin, OH 44074

Mary Helen Cochran Library
Sweet Briar College
Sweet Briar, VA 24595

Thomas Byrne Memorial Library
Spring Hill College
4000 Dauphin Street
Mobile, AL 36608

Everett Library
Queens College
1900 Selwyn Ave.
Charlotte, NC 28274-0001

Porter Henderson Library
Angelo State University
2601 West Ave. N.
San Angelo, TX 76909-0001

Mark O. Hatfield Library
Willamette University
900 State St.
Salem, OR 97301

David Bishop Skillman Library
Lafayette College
Easton, PA 18042

You are cordially invited
to become a charter member of the

FRIENDS
OF THE
LIBRARY

MESSIAH COLLEGE

The inaugural meeting of

FRIENDS OF THE LIBRARY

will be held

Saturday, May 22, 1993, at 7:00 P.M.

in the display area of the Messiah College Archives,

lower level of the Murray Learning Resources Center.

Guest Speaker

Dr. Robert Sider

Dickinson College professor and Erasmus scholar,

will speak about the purposes and privileges of a Friends group.

We look forward to seeing you.

RSVP by May 7 to Jonathan Lauer, Library Director, (717) 691-6006.

Friends of the Oberlin College Library

The Oberlin College Library

The **Main Library**, built in 1974, houses the majority of the Library's collections, including those in social sciences and humanities fields, mathematics and computer science. Modern in design, colorful and varied in decor, the building offers attractive places for study, research, and social interaction.

Designed by architect Robert Venturi as part of the 1977 addition to the Allen Art Museum, the **Art Library** houses collections in fine arts and architectural history.

The **Conservatory Library**, with collections in music and music history, was originally constructed in 1964 and renovated in 1988 when the first phase of an attractive 10,000 square foot addition designed by Gunnar Birkerts and Associates was completed. It is one of the nation's leading music libraries.

The **Science Library** in Kettering Hall and **Physics Reading Room** in the Wright Physics Building contain collections in the natural sciences.

Oberlin College Library holdings

Catalogued volumes:	1,137,000
Subscriptions:	3,800
Government documents:	386,000
Microtext items:	343,000
Sound recordings:	47,000

The true university of these days is a collection of books.
—Thomas Carlyle

A Library is not a luxury. It is one of the necessities of life.
—Henry Ward Beecher

The Library and the Friends: A Worthwhile Partnership

Oberlin has long had one of the nation's outstanding arts college libraries. The superb quality of our library system has been made possible not only through strong support from the College, but also through the generosity of countless friends and benefactors. The Friends of the Oberlin College Library, an organization formally established in November 1991, is continuing that rich heritage of support.

What Are Friends For?

Although relatively new, the Friends of the Library have already proved successful in:

Providing financial support that significantly strengthens the collections and services of the library beyond what would otherwise be possible. In the first five years of their existence the Friends have raised approximately $140,000. Most of those funds are being used to purchase new materials for the collections, including major scholarly sets and titles in new curricular areas. Purchases have included not only books but also videocassettes and materials in computerized formats.

Sponsoring programs that enrich the cultural life of the community. Past programs have included lectures by Geoffrey Ward '62, principal author of the PBS television series on the Civil War; syndicated columnist Carl T. Rowan '47; former Director of Libraries William A. Moffett; Nien Cheng, author of a best-selling memoir of the Chinese Cultural Revolution; Obie-award-winning dramatist Romulus Linney '53; Johnnetta Cole '57, President of Spelman College; and Oberlin's President Nancy Schrom Dye.

Stimulating greater awareness of books as objects and as tangible bearers of heritage. Workshops, exhibitions and lectures regularly focus on topics in the book arts.

Organizing activities for the enjoyment and benefit of members. Friends dinners and receptions provide enjoyable occasions for celebrating the importance of the Library, expressing appreciation for those who support it, and bringing together people of common interests.

Benefits of Membership

Membership in the Friends brings tangible rewards:

Friends receive the *Library Perspectives* newsletter as well as other information about the library and the activities of the Friends, including announcements and invitations to exhibitions, lectures, and other events. Members also receive occasional publications, such as the lectures delivered by Geoffrey Ward, Johnnetta Cole, and Nancy Dye.

Friends are entitled to library borrowing privileges.

Friends enjoy the fellowship of people who share their interest in books, book collecting, and the life of the mind.

Most of all, members of the **Friends of the Oberlin College Library have the satisfaction of knowing that they are helping to maintain and strengthen not only Oberlin's outstanding library,** but also the process that marks an Oberlin education.

Not Just a Worthy Cause

Today, more than ever, the library needs the support and partnership of people who understand its fundamental importance for education at Oberlin.

I hope you will join the faculty, staff, students, alumni, and others whose enthusiastic efforts are insuring the success of the Friends of the Oberlin College Library.

Come and take part. It's not just a worthy cause—it's one you'll also enjoy.

—Ray English, Director of Libraries

Friends Bookplate

The bookplate reproduced on the cover of this brochure is placed in all titles acquired for the library from Friends of the Library funds.

Friends of the Oberlin College Library

MEMBERSHIP CATEGORIES:

☐ $1 Student   ☐ $25 Friend   ☐ $50 Associate   ☐ $500 Patron

☐ $5 Recent Graduate   ☐ $30 Couple   ☐ $100 Sponsor   ☐ $1000 Benefactor

Enclosed is my 1997-98 Friends membership contribution of $ _____

CREDIT CARD PAYMENT   Card Number _____ Expiration Date _____

Signature _____ ☐ Mastercard ☐ Visa

Please inform me if my company will match my membership contribution.

My company is _____

Name _____

Street or P.O. Box _____

City _____

State _____ Zip _____

Your membership contribution is tax deductible.

PLEASE RETURN THIS CARD WITH YOUR MEMBERSHIP CONTRIBUTION.
MAKE YOUR CHECK PAYABLE TO OBERLIN COLLEGE.

FISCAL YEAR JULY 1 THROUGH JUNE 30

If you would like to join the FRIENDS OF THE SWEET BRIAR COLLEGE LIBRARY, please send the information requested below to FRIENDS OF THE LIBRARY, P.O. BOX G, SWEET BRIAR, VA 24595.

Name _____

Street _____

City _____ State _____ Zip _____

Telephone _____

Please check the class of membership desired:

☐ Regular	$ 25 per year	☐ Founding	$250 or more per year
☐ Supporting/Family	$ 35 per year	☐ Life	$3,000 payable over six years
☐ Sustaining	$ 50 per year	☐ Sweet Briar Student	$5 per year
☐ Benefactor	$100 per year	☐ Alumnae Clubs	$30 per year

Checks made payable to SWEET BRIAR COLLEGE are deductible for income tax purposes.

FRIENDS OF THE SWEET BRIAR COLLEGE LIBRARY

You are cordially invited to become an annual member of The Friends of The Library.

The purpose of FRIENDS organization is:

a) To encourage understanding of the work of Sweet Briar College's Mary Helen Cochran Library and its branches and to further a realization of the present and future importance of the Library to the College's advancement.

b) To attract to the College Library through gifts or bequests, new resources including funds, books, manuscripts, and other appropriate material beyond what the College budget can provide.

c) To serve as a medium through which The Friends of The Library members may become acquainted and share their enthusiasm for books.

Please complete the reverse side of this card and, using the envelope provided, return it with your check made payable to SWEET BRIAR COLLEGE.

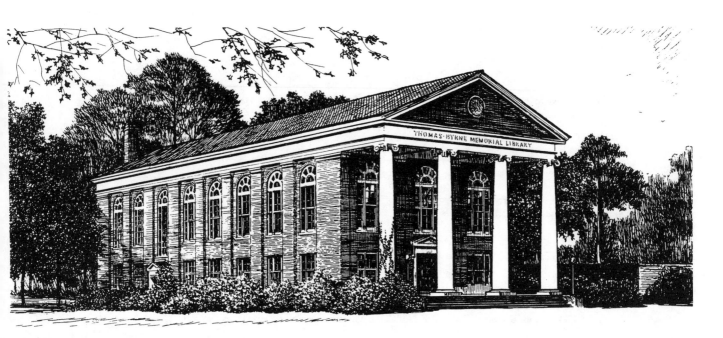

Your Special
Invitation
to
Become
a

Friend
of the
Spring Hill
College
Library

At the time of the dedication of the Thomas Byrne Memorial Library on June 1, 1930, during Spring Hill's Centennial celebration, a Mobile Press Register editorial said:

> Mr. Byrne, who had an intimate understanding of what the College is doing today and of its constantly broadening usefulness as a great educational center, could not have left a more substantial or enduring memorial.... This great modern scientific Library is not only a beautiful monument to a thoughtful citizen and a useful factor in the life of a great institution, but is destined to become a permanent center of culture in this community, enlightening and brightening the lives of many generations to come.

The library has indeed endured during these sixty years and has enlightened the lives of several generations of students and members of the community.

The Friends of the Spring Hill College Library is an organization now being formed to help perpetuate that tradition. Several founding members of the Friends, Charlotte and Sam Eichold, Charmane and Lloyd May and members of Huisking family through their foundation, have made it possible to preserve the College's rare books and manuscripts by funding the creation of a Rare Book Room. However, with rapid changes taking place in the technology of communication, cataloging, publishing, and every area of library management, much remains to be done to bring the Library into the 21st century.

You are invited to become a member, to share your ideas and to become part of the Library's progress and improvement.

THE PURPOSE OF THE FRIENDS

I

To sustain, strengthen and further develop library facilities, collections and services.

II

To provide an opportunity for interested individuals to come together out of common interest in Spring Hill College and its library.

III

To enhance involvement in and enthusiasm for the literary world.

IV

To encourage bequests and gifts of books, manuscripts and financial support for materials and projects that exceed the resources of the library budget.

V

To assist in special library projects.

VI

To promote library/community ties that enlarge the service capacity of the library and promote effective use of libraries.

----✂----------✂----------✂----------✂----------✂- --------✂----------✂----------✂----------✂----------✂--------✂--------✂--------✂------✂-----

The Friends of the Spring Hill College Library
in the Thomas Byrne Memorial Building

I/We wish to join The Friends of the Spring Hill College Library as indicated below:

❏ SHC Student	$10.00	❏ Individual	$25.00	❏ Sustaining	$250.00
❏ SHC Faculty/Staff	$15.00	❏ Family	$40.00	❏ Corporate	$500.00
❏ SHC Alumni	$20.00	❏ Patron	$100.00	❏ Lifetime *	$1000.00

All levels include borrowing privileges.

Name _____ Phone (_____)_____

Address _____

City, State, Zip_____

❏ I would like to serve on a committee.   *Payable in increments*

Your tax-deductible check may be made payable to Spring Hill College with a notation for Friends of the Library. Send check along with this membership form to the Development Office, Friends of the Spring Hill College Library, 4000 Dauphin Street, Mobile, AL 36608-1791. Telephone (205) 460-2381.

Everett Library

The mural, composed of some 250,000 pieces of colored stone and Italian tile, stands five feet in height by sixty feet in length and rests above the entrance of Everett Library. ■ Edmund D. Lewandowski, who executed mosaic murals for the Milwaukee Memorial Center and Marquette University, designed and executed the Queens College mural which is a representation of the fields of knowledge included in the materials of the college library. It is given unity by the relationship between the first panel, the last panel and the central section. The Alpha and the Omega of the first and last panels are related to the central section which presents a number of

religious symbols signifying the Christian affiliation of the college in its institutional life as well as in its educational ideals. ■ Reading the mural from left to right, the first group of four panels depicts mathematics. The second group of panels symbolizes astronomy and physics. ■ The next group of nine panels symbolizes the humanities and includes references to the social sciences. The succeeding group of panels represents various aspects of religion. The next panel is devoted to law and government with the balances and gavel representing law, and the eagle representing government. ■ The following group of panels represents various forms of chemistry. Two panels at the right of these typify industry. The next group of symbols is related to biology, physiology, medicine and nursing. ■ The three panels with the names Plato, Socrates and Aristotle represent both philosophy and the cultural heritage from the Greeks. The last panel is Omega referring the first panel and the center section on religion.

Non-Profit Organization
U.S. Postage
PAID
Charlotte, NC
Permit Number 769

Friends of the Library
Queens College
1900 Selwyn Ave.
Charlotte, NC 28274

QUEENS COLLEGE

Friends of the Library

QUEENS COLLEGE

In 1971, a group of Charlotte men and women organized the Friends of Everett Library with a goal

of broadening the influence and usefulness of Everett Library and enriching the cultural life of the Charlotte area.

Each spring, the Friends of the Library sponsor the annual Book and Author dinner and luncheon which bring noted authors

who read and discuss their recent writings.
The Friends also sponsor a program in the fall.
Membership, which is open to all, helps support
Everett Library with gifts of literary and scholarly

materials, equipment, and furnishings. The Friends also encourage contributions to the Everett Library endowment funds

which provide continuing support to the Library. Three endowed funds initiated by the Friends are:

The **E**verett **L**ibrary **E**ndowment   **T**he **H**elen & **F**reeman **J**ones **E**ndowed **B**ook **F**und   **T**he **W**alter **S**pearman **F**und.

FRIEND: $15/year (*Single*) $25/year (*Couple*)

Benefits include: use of Everett Library, including borrowing privileges; invitations to all Friends of the Library events; Friends of the Library newsletter; and an option to purchase one ticket per member to the Book and Author Event.

PATRON: $100/year

Benefits include: all the benefits of the Friend level; option to purchase two tickets to the Book and Author Event; and an invitation to the annual Patrons' Party.

BENEFACTOR: $250/year

Benefits include: all the benefits of the Patron level; and two new books will be added to Everett Library, each bearing a bookplate in honor of the Benefactor or in honor or memory of the Benefactor's designee.

EVERETT SOCIETY: $500/year

Benefits include: all the benefits of the Patron level; plus five new books will be added to Everett Library, each bearing a bookplate in honor of the Everett Society member or in honor or memory of the member's designee.

RENA HARRELL SOCIETY:*
one gift of **$1000**

Benefits include:
Life membership in the Friends of the Library; all benefits of the Patron level; plus a significant part of the gift will be placed in the Everett Library Endowment to provide ongoing support to the library. An artist-designed bookplate will be placed in one book each year for the life of the member in his or her honor or in honor or memory of a designee; and a framed copy of the bookplate will be presented at the Annual Meeting.

* *(This Society honors the memory of Rena Chambers Harrell, Librarian at Queens College from 1926 to 1956. Miss Harrell, a 1912 graduate of Queens, directed the college library and devoted her life to building a solid library collection for the college.)*

Application

T H A N K Y O U

Name_____

Address_____

City_____

State_____Zip_____

Please check the appropriate Membership Category located to the right and mail to: **Friends of the Library/Queens College 1900 Selwyn Ave. Charlotte, NC 28274**

Friend: Single	$15/year
Couple	$25/year
Patron	$100/year
Benefactor	$250/year
Everett Society	$500/year
Rena Harrell Society	$1000

Thank you for supporting the Friends of the Library. Membership dues are tax deductible as allowed by law. A receipt will be mailed to you along with your membership card in three to four weeks.

Friends

OF THE PORTER
HENDERSON LIBRARY
AND WEST TEXAS
COLLECTION

Friends

BOX 11013, ASU STATION
SAN ANGELO, TX 76909

OF THE PORTER
HENDERSON LIBRARY
AND WEST TEXAS
COLLECTION

Members' Benefits

Library borrowing privileges

Interlibrary loan privileges

Newsletter

Invitations to events sponsored by the
Friends and/or Library and WTC

Spouse may share membership benefits

Group rate Internet services
are available

*Preserving the past
...for the future*

Become a Friend of the Porter Henderson Library and West Texas Collection

The *Friends* welcome anyone interested in building the excellence of the ASU Library and its Collections. The *Friends* are dedicated to helping the Library and the WTC achieve their goal of excellence.

The purposes of this organization are:

- to enrich the resources; to preserve, enhance, and promote the collections, services, programs, and facilities of the Library and WTC,

- to promote activities to make the Library resources and services more widely known, and

- to develop understanding and support of the Library and WTC.

The *Friends* comprise a new organization with membership open to anyone interested in the support, promotion, and growth of the Library and WTC. Your gift will go toward such items as books, seminars, technical assistance, and equipment necessary to ensure that the Library and WTC continue to serve your information needs and that of the ASU community and the entire West Texas area.

Contributions are tax-deductible to the extent allowed by law.

YES! Count me as a Friend.

Individuals *(spouse may also be included)*

☐ Founders Club	$2500
☐ Library Fellow	$1000
☐ Benefactor	$500
☐ Patron	$250
☐ Sustaining	$100
☐ Contributing	$50
☐ Regular	$30
☐ Student	$15

Businesses

☐ Corporate Partner	$1000
☐ Preferred Stockholder	$500
☐ Investors	$250

☐ My/our employer(s) will match this gift.
Enclose company matching gift form.

Name _____
Address _____
City _____
State _____ Zip _____
Phone _____
Email _____

Thank you!

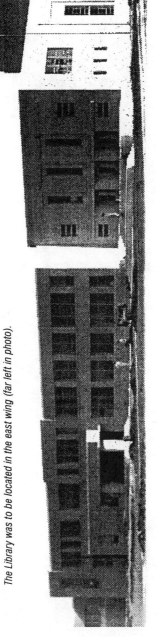

The Main Building, San Angelo College, under construction circa 1947.
The Library was to be located in the east wing (far left in photo).

WILLAMETTE
UNIVERSITY

*Friends
of the
Library*

SPRING
BANQUET

March 11, 1998
6:00 p.m.
Cat Cavern

In 1973, a group of Willamette faculty and librarians founded the Friends of the Library. Their aims were:

❖ to enrich the holdings of the Willamette Library;

❖ to foster interest in, and support of, the Library;

❖ to enhance the cultural life of the campus and community by sponsoring special programs in the Library.

If you are interested in joining the Friends of the Library, please pick up a membership form before you leave this evening or contact Dayna at (503) 370-6312.

Willamette University
Friends of the Library
900 State Street
Salem, Oregon 97301
(503) 370-6312

UPCOMING EVENTS

March 13 - Poetry Readings
Barbara Drake & Charles Goodrich
(7:30 p.m. Hatfield Room)

April 6 - Civil War historian, James McPherson. Tickets available to FOL members by calling Sheri Martin (370-6552) by April 3.
(8:00 p.m. Smith Auditorium)

April 10 - Poetry Readings
Clem Starck & Robert Peterson
(7:30 p.m. Hatfield Room)

April 19 & 26 - Preview Talks 1998 Season of Plays Oregon Shakespeare Festival
(2:00 p.m. Hatfield Room)

May 1 - Poetry Readings
Clem Starck's poetry class
(7:30 p.m. Hatfield Room)

PROGRAM

Invocation

Charles Wallace
Chaplain
Associate Professor of Religion

Welcome

Bill Braden
Professor of English
President, Friends of the Library

Introductions

Special Guest: Mrs. Nancy B. Hunt

Larry R. Oberg
University Librarian

Disappearing Books

Albert and Virginia Furtwangler

Closing Remarks

Bill Braden

OUR SPEAKERS

Albert Furtwangler received his B.A. from Amherst College and his M.A. and Ph.D. from Cornell University. He taught at Mount Allison University for 25 years and is the author of several noteworthy books.

Al's Writings:

◆ *The Authority of Publius: A Reading of the Federalist Papers*
◆ *American Silhouettes: Rhetorical Identities of the Founders*
◆ *Assassin on Stage: Brutus, Hamlet, and the Death of Lincoln*
◆ *Acts of Discovery: Visions of America in the Lewis and Clark Journals*
◆ *Answering Chief Seattle*

Virginia Furtwangler, who writes under the name Ann Copeland, received her B.A. from College of New Rochelle, her M.A. from Catholic University of America, and her Ph.D. from Cornell University. Ginny has taught at a number of universities in the U.S. and Canada as visiting fiction writer. She currently holds the Hallie Brown Ford Chair in English at Willamette University.

Ann's Writings:

◆ *At Peace*
◆ *The Back Room*
◆ *Earthen Vessels*
◆ *The Golden Thread*
◆ *Strange Bodies on a Stranger Shore*
◆ *Season of Apples*
◆ *The ABC's of Writing Fiction*

Ginny and Al enjoy ballroom dancing and love being in Oregon. Ginny writes, "We don't read each other's books until they're in print. It's made for a good marriage."

MUSIC PROVIDED BY

Schubert Quartet

Janel Lamb, *violin*
Ariel Kimball, *violin*
Laurie Braun, *viola*
Derek Linke, *cello*

❖

Eine kleine Nachtmusik
(*Mozart*)
Serenade Op. 48
(*Tchaikowsky*)
Quartet in D Minor
(*Schubert*)

RIENDS

of the

KILLMAN

IBRARY

LAFAYETTE COLLEGE

Benefits of Membership

Although the primary benefit of membership is the satisfaction that comes from making a lasting contribution to learning, Friends enjoy the following special benefits:

Borrowing privileges — Every member receives a library card that entitles him or her to borrow books from the library.

Publications — Members receive the Friends newsletter, *Cur Non*, published twice a year, along with exhibition posters and special occasional publications.

Exhibits — Friends are invited to attend exhibit openings, receptions and other events.

Lectures — Friends receive special notification of brown bag lunch programs that include lectures by faculty and other guests, and of video series such as "The Story of English."

Annual Meeting — Friends are invited to attend the annual meeting in the spring, which includes dinner and a special lecture.

An Invitation to Join

We invite you to become a Friend of Skillman Library by returning the enclosed card with your gift. Your support will help enhance this already significant collection and help demonstrate the importance of libraries in the modern age. When we receive your completed card, your name will be entered on the membership rolls and you will receive your first issue of *Cur Non*. Please make your gift payable to Lafayette College. Gifts are tax deductible to the extent allowed by law.

For additional information, please write or call the Secretary, Friends of the Skillman Library, Skillman Library, Lafayette College, Easton, PA 18042-1797. Phone: (215) 250-5151.

The Friends of the Skillman Library

The Friends of the Skillman Library is an association of individuals dedicated to the advancement of this growing collection of books, periodicals, manuscripts, archives and other important bibliographic materials. Founded in 1964, the Friends now number 450 members, including faculty, students, alumni/ae, community residents, bibliophiles and others who share a special interest in the development of this 400,000-volume library at the heart of the Lafayette College campus.

Through gifts and membership dues, the Friends have helped to fund special acquisitions for the library, ranging from rare books to electronic technologies. Recent purchases made possible by the Friends have included letters of the Marquis de Lafayette; first editions of the works of Charles Dickens, John Dos Passos and other literary figures; state-of-the-art video viewing equipment; and a popular CD-ROM data file. In addition, the Friends have supported special projects to make the Library's resources better known both locally and nationally. The Stephen Crane centennial celebration and the cataloging project for the Marquis de Lafayette book collection are two such projects. The Friends also sponsor lectures, receptions and exhibition openings throughout the year for the benefit of both the college and the community.

Woodcut initials are from Tommaso Porcacchi's L'ISOLE PIV FAMOSE DEL MONDO (Venice, 1590) in the Skillman Library's Rare Book Collection.

Program Ideas

Mark O. Hatfield Library
Willamette University
900 State St.
Salem, OR 97301

Murray Learning Resources Center
Messiah College
Grantham, PA 17027-9990

Folke Berndotte Memorial Library
Gustavus Adolphus College
800 W. College Ave.
St. Peter, MN 56082

Everett Library
Queens College
1900 Selwyn Ave.
Charlotte, NC 28274-0001

Cullom-Davis Library
Bradley University
1501 W. Bradley Avenue
Peoria, IL 61625

Mikkelsen Library
Augustana College
Sioux Falls, SD 57197-0001

Ralph M. Besse Library
Ursuline College
2550 Lander Road
Cleveland, OH 44124-4398

Willamette University
Friends of the Library
Annual Book Sale

Thursday, February 5, 1998
9:00 a.m. - 5:00 p.m.
(Opens to the public at 1:00 p.m.)

24-Hour Study at the
Mark O. Hatfield Library

**Great selection of books
Hardbacks $1.00
Paperbacks $.50
Vintage LPs $.10 each or 12/$1.00**

**Book donations accepted through
January 19 - please bring your
books to the Hatfield Library**

Questions? Contact Dayna at 370-6312

A Special Invitation

The honor of your presence is requested at
Evening of Elegance ~ A Royal Affair
Dinner
Dancing
Silent and Live Auctions

Saturday, the eighth of November
Nineteen hundred and ninety-seven
Five-thirty o'clock in the evening

Grand Ballroom
Radisson Hotel South
Bloomington, Minnesota

Sponsored by
Gustavus Library Associates

Reservations required
Black tie optional

Funds from *Evening of Elegance ~ A Royal Affair* are designated for Folke Bernadotte
Memorial Library on the campus of Gustavus Adolphus College, Saint Peter, Minnesota.

Name _____

Address _____

City _____ State _____ ZIP _____

Telephone _____ / _____

We will attend *Evening of Elegance ~ A Royal Affair* as:

_____ Corporate table ($1250 per table of ten persons).
__ __ Corporate table ($1000 per table of eight persons).
_____ Benefactors $300 per person ($262.50 tax deductible).
_____ Patrons $150 per person ($112.50 tax deductible).
_____ Guests $85 per person ($47.50 tax deductible).
_____ We are unable to attend.

Enclosed please find our contribution in the amount of $_____.

Our check in the amount of $_____, payable to Gustavus Adolphus College, is enclosed.

Corporate sponsors, benefactors and patrons will be acknowledged in the dinner program.

Reservations are requested by October 24.

Special overnight rates available at Radisson Hotel South, 612/893-8435.

Evening of Elegance
A Royal Affair

November 8, 1997
Radisson Hotel South ~ Bloomington, Minnesota

a benefit for Folke Bernadotte Memorial Library
Gustavus Adolphus College ~ Saint Peter, Minnesota

Contents

Note: The IRS has instituted a "special emphasis program" regarding contributions where the donor receives a benefit or privilege in return for the contribution. Only the excess of the total contribution over the fair market value of the benefit received is deductible as a charitable contribution deduction.

Thank you for your support of Gustavus Adolphus College through this benefit sponsored by Gustavus Library Associates. Funds from *Evening of Elegance* are designated for enhancing the teaching and research resources of Folke Bernadotte Memorial Library.

Silent auction bidding is done by placing your bidding number beside the amount you wish to bid for a particular item. Bids must be made in minimum increments of one dollar.

Trumpets will herald the closing of the silent auction at the end of the soup course.

When the silent auction closes, claim checks will be delivered to the highest bidders during the dessert course.

Cashiers will be located outside the ballroom until the conclusion of the evening. Payment may be made by VISA, MasterCard, cash or check payable to Gustavus Adolphus College. Items are to be taken with you unless otherwise indicated. Winners contact donors where appropriate.

Photography in the auction program is by Stan Waldhauser unless otherwise noted.

FRIENDS of the LIBRARY

QUEENS COLLEGE

cordially invite you to the

PATRONS
RECEPTION

Monday, March 9th

6:00 pm

Burwell Hall

Please reply by March 3rd to:
Kathy McCollum   377-2324
Ginni Durham 377-0581

Fourth Annual

Mid-America's

Book & Paper Fair

• Sponsored by • Friends of Cullom-Davis Library •

September 27, 1997

Old Book Evaluation Clinic
(2 books per person)
10:00 a.m. to 3:00 p.m.

➜ Schedule of Events ⬅

9:00 Book Fair Opening

📖 Public Lectures:

    10:00 Everything You Always Wanted to Know
           about Books but Were Afraid to Ask

    11:00 Collecting Paper

    11:30 Books on the Internet

    12:30 Postcard Collecting and Evaluation

     1:30 You Wrote a Great Story - Now What?

     2:30 Gold in Your Attic

📖 Childrens Corner: Children only or accompanied by an
    adult to purchase books.
    Storytelling: 10:30, 11:30, 1:30 and 2:30

📖 Old Book Clinic (2 books per person)
    10:00 a.m. to 3:00 p.m.

✍ Author Signing:
    10:00 a.m. to 12:00 p.m.

• Beardstown Ladies	• Susan Guengerich
• Jack Bradley	• Robert Hellenga
• Steve Burgauer	• Fred Novotny
• David B. Cheesebrough	• William Reynolds
• Fox Ellis	• Ed Sutkowski
• David Gent	• David Walker

    1:00 p.m. to 3:00 p.m.

• Nancy Atherton	• David Gent
• Jack Bradley	• Susan Guengerich
• Steve Burgauer	• Mike Rucker
• Dorothy Cannell	• Ed Sutkowski
• David B. Cheesebrough	• Cinda Thompson
• Philip Jose Farmer	• Michael Westheim

4:00 Book Fair Closing (Schedule changes could occur)

A Winter's Tale

Mikkelsen Library
Augustana College
2001 S. Summit
Sioux Falls, SD 57197

Augustana Library Associates presents

A Winter's Tale:
In The Good Old Summertime.
Saturday, February 7, 1998, 8:00 p.m.

Mikkelsen Library

Sandra Looney, Mistress of Ceremonies

Gary Pederson, banjo
Dick Hanson, guitar

Readers
Dave Nelson
Valerie Putnam
Don Levsen
Josephine Jones
Ron Robinson
Nancy Tieszen

A reception will follow

$12.00 General Admission
$10.00 Library Associates

For information call 605-336-4921

RSVP by January 30

A Winter's Tale:

In The Good Old Summertime

My check for $_____ is enclosed
please make checks payable to Augustana Library Associates

Name _____

Phone _____

Number of persons _____

For information call 336-4921

The Augustana Library Associates presents

A Winter's Tale:
In The Good Old Summertime

Summertime
from Porgy and Bess

Summertime
And the living is easy
Fish are jumpin'
And the cotton is high

Your Daddy's rich
And your mama's good lookin'
So hush little baby now
don't you cry

One of these mornin's
You're gonna rise up singin'
You're gonna spread your wings
And take to the sky

But til that mornin'
Ain't nothin' can harm you
With your daddy and your mammy
standin' by

~~Lyrics by DuBose Heyward

A Winter's Tale: In The Good Old Summertime

Sandra Looney, Mistress of Ceremonies

Gary Pederson & Dick Hanson
  Medley of Jazz and Blues

Don Levsen
  Pied Beauty, by Gerard Manley Hopkins

  Summer-time, from _Farmer Boy_,
    by Laura Ingalls Wilder

  On Warm Summer Nights, by David Bengston

Josephine Jones
  Weather Report: June 30, by Kathleen Norris

  Planting, by Cinda Thompson

  The Fish, by Elizabeth Bishop

Ron Robinson
  The Alder Fork—A Fishing Idyl from _A Sand County Almanac_
    by Alde Leopold

  Seattle-Bremerton Ferry and The Cornstalk Fiddle,
    by Ron Robinson

Gary Pederson & Dick Hanson
>   *Take Me Home, Country Roads* by John Denver

Nancy Tieszen
>   *I Wandered Lonely as a Cloud,* by William Wordsworth

>   *Hollyhocks,* by Kathleene West

>   *Perennials,* by Kathleen Norris

Dave Nelson
>   *Birches,* by Robert Frost

>   *Summer, from <u>Lake Wobegon Days,</u>* by Garrison Keillor

Val Putnam
>   *The Groundhog,* by Richard Eberhart

>   *Excerpts from <u>The Circle of Quiet</u>,* by Madeleine L'Engle

Ron Robinson
>   *Casey at the Bat,* by Ernest Thayer

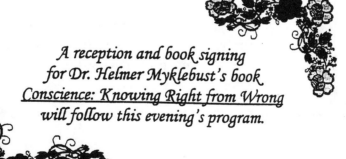

*A reception and book signing
for Dr. Helmer Myklebust's book
<u>Conscience: Knowing Right from Wrong</u>
will follow this evening's program.*

The Friends and Guests of Ursuline College's
Ralph M. Besse Library are invited to attend
the musical comedy

"Godspell"

Friday, March 29, 1996

Beginning. . .
> *The evening will begin at 6 p.m.*
> *with an optional dinner at Gamekeeper's*
> *Taverne. We will sit together and choose*
> *from four meals at a special price of $12.*
> *(Friends will make the arrangements, but*
> *each attendee will pay in person).*

" Godspell"
> *Chagrin Valley Little Theatre - 8 p.m.*

And on into the night. . .
> *A dessert reception in the Rivers Room*
> *of the Chagrin Valley Little Theatre*

> *We hope you will join us for this enjoyable*
> *evening benefit with "Friends"*

Cost is $15 per person for theater and dessert reception.
Please return RSVP and payment by March 18.
For more details call 646-8184.

Newsletters

Charles E. Shain Library
Connecticut College
270 Mohegan Ave.
New London, CT 06320-4196

David Bishop Skillman Library
Lafayette College
Easton, PA 18042

L.A. Beeghly Library
Ohio Wesleyan University
43 University Ave.
Delaware, OH 43015

Jessie Ball DuPont Library
University of the South
Sewanee, TN 37375-1000

Oberlin College Library
Oberlin College
Oberlin, OH 44074

Margaret Clapp Library
Wellesley College
106 Central Street
Wellesley, MA

1998 Friends of the Connecticut College Library Winter Newsletter

WINTER EXHIBITION:
ANOTHER CORNER OF PARNASSUS:
WILLIAM MEREDITH AND THE 1997
NATIONAL BOOK AWARD FOR POETRY
JANUARY 5 – MARCH 31, 1998

Cover of paperback edition of Meredith's
Effort at Speech; *photograph by Resurreccion*
Frink

On November 18 Professor Emeritus William Meredith received the prestigious National Book Award for *Effort at Speech*, a collection of eleven previously unpublished poems and a selection from his eight books published between 1944 and 1987. To celebrate this event an exhibition on Meredith's literary career is on view in the Charles E. Shain Library through March 31. The exhibition spans Meredith's career as poet and teacher, from his Princeton senior thesis on Robert Frost to the November award. Books, inscriptions, periodicals and pictures are interspersed with letters from the Library's Meredith Papers to provide a glimpse of the literary life.

Two bronze sculptures are on view: a portrait of Meredith as a young man and a winged *Pegasus*, the token of the 1979 International Vaptsarov Prize for Literature presented to Meredith by the Government of Bulgaria. The exhibition includes photographs of the memorable 1996 poetry reading, attended by many Friends, on the occasion of Shain Library's 20th anniversary. The title of the exhibition is derived from James Merrill's congratulatory letter (on display), sent to Meredith after he received the 1988 Pulitzer Prize for *Partial Accounts*.

Pegasus is on loan from its owner, but all other items on display are drawn from the William Meredith Collection, a virtually complete collection of his published work (including single poems reprinted in more than 150 anthologies or issues of periodicals), and the William Meredith Papers. *For more information please call exhibition curator Brian Rogers at (860) 439-2654.*

CHARLES E. SHAIN LIBRARY
GREER MUSIC LIBRARY

Charles E. Shain Library

JOHN MERRILL PUBLISHES MEETING THE SUBMARINE CHALLENGE: A SHORT HISTORY OF THE NAVAL UNDERWATER SYSTEMS CENTER

The Friends of the
Connecticut College Library

Connie V. Dowell
Dean of Information Services and
Librarian of the College

Brian Rogers
Special Collections Librarian and
Newsletter Editor

Charles E. Shain Library
Greer Music Library
Connecticut College
270 Mohegan Avenue
New London, CT
06320-4196
Telephone (860) 439-2654
E-mail: bdrog@conncoll.edu

January, 1998

Longtime Friend John Merrill has seen the result of years of research and writing take shape in the form of a 372-page history of the NUSC recently published by the Department of the Navy. An electronic engineer, John was head of the Submarine Electromagnetic Systems Department at the time of his retirement, and had been program manager for the development of the extremely low frequency (ELF) radio wave global submarine communication system. Although the book contains much technical material, it may be appreciated by anyone with an interest in submarines and naval history. The brief historical background of the Fort Trumbull site is particularly interesting in view of the possibility that it may become a Connecticut state park.

"The site of NUSC's New London facility included structures from nearly every generation of its more than two hundred years of military use. The 1790 Revolutionary War blockhouse (Building 42) and Fort Trumbull itself (Building 32) are listed on the National Register of Historic Places." (from "The New London Background," page 9.)

A native of Buffalo, John has been a resident of Waterford for many years and is a frequent visitor to Shain Library. The book is being distributed to research libraries throughout the country as part of the depository program of the U.S. Government Printing Office. We congratulate John and co-author Lionel D. Wyld on their impressive achievement. A copy may be examined in the Palmer Room, where it is part of our New London history collection. (Call Brian Rogers at 439-2654 to be sure the Palmer Room is open when you would like to visit.)

Postcard view of Fort Trumbull Block House; from New London postcard collection, Charles E. Shain Library.

Oona & Charlie

Christmas card from Oona and Charlie Chaplin to Louis Sheaffer, 1972

PURCHASE OF OONA O'NEILL CHAPLIN LETTERS Made Possible by the Friends of the Library

We are pleased to report that the purchase of a unique collection of 126 letters written by the late Lady Oona Chaplin to Louis Sheaffer was completed in 1997. Because the Sheaffer estate was willing to accept payment in installments over more than two years, it was possible to fund this purchase with the annual contributions of the Friends of the Library, supplemented with income from the Friends endowment. We are grateful for the continuing generosity of our members which has made this extraordinary purchase possible.

Her letters make clear how important Lady Chaplin's support and friendship was to Louis Sheaffer in writing the two-volume biography of her famous father Eugene. We are grateful to the executors of the Sheaffer estate for giving us the first opportunity to

acquire this immensely significant correspondence for the Sheaffer-O'Neill Collection.

One of the most frequently used parts of the Sheaffer-O'Neill Collection in recent months has been the photograph file. Since the last newsletter, images have been supplied to the producers of a PBS documentary and accompanying book, "The Irish in America"; to the Pittsburgh Public Theater and the Madison (Wisconsin) Repertory Theater for playbills; to the Zimmerli Art Museum at Rutgers University, and to a Canadian author for his psychological biography of O'Neill to be published this year by Yale University Press.

A NOTE ON THE TYPOGRAPHY

This newsletter is set in Adobe Garamond, modeled in 1989 by Robert Slimbach on 16th century designs researched at the Plantin-Moretus Museum in Antwerp. The many 20th century versions of Garamond are based on the designs of Claude Garamond (1480-1561), first used in books printed in Paris around 1532. Garamond's original fonts are in the French Imprimerie Nationale.

INFORMATION SOUGHT ON NEW LONDON COMPOSER FREDERICK COIT WIGHT

One of the special strengths of the Library's Special Collections is the history of New London. While much of the material dates back to the 18th century, including the first book printed in Connecticut and dozens of examples of work by New London printer Timothy Green, other holdings are of more recent origin. Among these is a collection of music materials by New London composer Frederick Coit Wight (1859-1933) consisting of libretti, scripts, orchestral and choral parts to his larger-scale works, and a number of his published songs. Wight was especially noted for his band marches, and several of these were performed in the presence of American presidents on ceremonial occasions. An active Rotarian, he composed "Hail, New London" in 1923 in honor of the New London Rotary Club.

In preparation for making the Wight Collection available to library users, Music Librarian Carolyn Johnson seeks information about Wight, his family, and his music. Among other things she would like to discover where his manuscripts are located. According to his obituary in *The Day* of December 23, 1933, he married Belle Brown, daughter of Dr. W. S. Brown. Their daughter, Nanette, married a George Bragaw, and they also had a daughter. If any reader is able to provide further information about Frederick Coit Wight or his descendants, please contact Carolyn Johnson, Music Librarian, at 439-2710, or Brian Rogers, Special Collections Librarian, at 439-2654.

ANOTHER CORNER OF PARNASSUS:

WILLIAM MEREDITH AND THE 1997 NATIONAL BOOK AWARD FOR POETRY

Charles E. Shain Library

Connecticut College

January 5–March 31, 1998

Exhibit supported by the Friends of the Library

YOUR MEMBERSHIP INVITED FOR 1998

■ *As another year begins*, we invite you to renew your membership in the Friends of the Connecticut College Library. To those who have recently done so, we sincerely thank you. We welcome new members at any time, and urge readers to let us know of anyone in our area who would enjoy a formal association with one of the New London area's major cultural resources.

■ *Membership contributions* are the primary source of financial support for the Department of Special Collections. They enable us to acquire rare books or other materials, and are used to pay any costs associated with public exhibitions, which are the most important way our holdings may be seen by the campus and the regional community. Member support enables the Library to offer public lectures from time to time, provides a scholarship award to a graduating senior or alumna/alumnus attending a graduate program in library and information studies, and underwrites the cost of this newsletter. With this issue we leave behind the format used since 1983 in favor of this fresh new look created for us by Susan Lindberg of the Office of Publications.

■ *The Palmer Room.* This attractive reading room on the second floor houses the personal libraries of George S. Palmer and his brother Elisha Loomis Palmer and other collections, and is the location of occasional lectures and receptions. The Room is normally open weekdays from 1 to 5 p.m. and members of the Friends are invited to make it their headquarters when visiting the Library for any reason. If you are visiting the Library specifically to use the Special Collections, it is advisable to make an appointment with Brian Rogers by calling 439-2654.

SPRING 1998   VOL. 9, NO. 2   THE FRIENDS OF SKILLMAN LIBRARY

Anthony Grafton to Speak at Annual Dinner Meeting

Anthony Grafton, a member of Princeton University's department of history, will speak on the topic "The History of Books and Readers" at the annual dinner of the Friends of Skillman Library on Thursday, April 30. Grafton has been widely praised for his distinguished writing about classical, Renaissance, and modern European cultures and about textual history. His latest book, *The Footnote: A Curious History* [1], has received enthusiastic acclaim and is the latest example of Grafton's rare ability to engage both general and more specialized audiences.

The holder of three degrees from the University of Chicago [2], Grafton has taught at Princeton since 1975 and has held two successive distinguished chairs in the history department [3]. He has received numerous honors and grants [4], including those from such foundations as Woodrow Wilson, Danforth, Fulbright-Hays, American Philosophical Society, American Council of Learned Societies, National Endowment for the Humanities, and Guggenheim. He has also received grants from German, Austrian, and French institutions as well as the British Academy. The *Los Angeles Times* gave him its prize for history in 1993.   *(continued on page 2)*

Spring Exhibit: Photographs by Martin J. Desht

The work of Pennsylvania photographer Martin J. Desht is featured in Skillman Library this semester. Two installations, one in the lobby gallery and the other in the Special Collections Reading Room, showcase Desht's work of the last decade and include photographs from his acclaimed "American Dream" series.

"Faces from an American Dream," on view in the Skillman lobby, is a photographic documentary that explores America's transition away from an industrial to a service economy, with particular emphasis on how this rapid social change has affected the lives of industrial workers, their towns, culture, and communities in Pennsylvania. The images hauntingly capture the landscape of abandoned factories and faces of former workers in the mill and mining towns of what was once the most industrialized state in the nation.

The American Dream project is a collaboration between Martin Desht and Lafayette Professor of History, Richard E. Sharpless. In 1989 Sharpless asked Desht, his neighbor in Raubsville, Pa., to take photographs for a book he was writing on the consequences of deindustrialization in Pennsylvania. Together Sharpless and Desht traveled the state, interviewing and photographing residents for whom the American Dream had become more like a nightmare with the onset of industrial abandonment.

Another side to Desht's work is reflected in
(continued on page 4)

Grafton

(continued from page 1)

In addition to his dozen books, notably *From Humanism to the Humanities: Education and the Liberal Arts in Fifteenth- and Sixteenth-Century Europe* (Harvard, 1986) and *Forgers and Critics: Creativity and Duplicity in Western Scholarship* (Princeton, 1990), as well as many [5] contributions in several languages to numerous collections and scholarly and popular publications, Grafton has written two important exhibition catalogues, both outgrowths of exhibitions he has curated [6].

He has been honored by invitations to deliver a number of distinguished lectures, both individually and as series, including the Thomas Spencer Jerome Lectures (American Academy in Rome and the University of Michigan, 1992), the J. H. Gray lectures (Cambridge University, 1995), the Rothschild Lecture in the History of Science (Harvard University, 1995), the Menahem Stern Lectures (Jerusalem, 1995), the E. A. Lowe Lectures in Palaeography and Kindred Subjects (Oxford University, 1996), and the Meyer Schapiro Lectures (Columbia University, 1997).

In his erudite, graceful study of the footnote, Grafton contends that footnotes can constitute a "high form of literary art" and can even be entertaining. His witty, wide-ranging study moves freely from the Renaissance through David Hume, Pierre Bayle, and Edward Gibbon (the acknowledged master of footnotes) to the present. The study has received such accolades as "a substantive" study that presents the footnote as "fairly stagger[ing] under the weight of significance" (*New York Times*) and "the most recent intellectual entertainment from one of the most learned and enjoyable scholars now at work" (*Washington Post*). *TLS* called this study "far-roaming," "urbane," "wittily dry and slightly sly," and "wholly entertaining."

Grafton is currently working on five additional books, including a history of Princeton University, as well as three future projects, including a history of Renaissance Europe and one on "proof-correction" from the Renaissance to the Enlightenment.

Footnotes:

1 (Harvard Univ. Press, 1997).
2 A.B., 1971; A.M., 1972; Ph.D., 1975, all in history, of course.
3 Andrew W. Mellon Chair from 1988-93, Dodge Professor from 1993 to the present.
4 This list is so impressive that it has been moved back to the text of this article for greater emphasis. Sorry for the extra, utterly wasted footnote.
5 Approximately 100 essays, book chapters, and review-essays.
6 (with others) *New Worlds, Ancient Texts* (Harvard Univ. Press, 1992); (with others) *Rome Reborn: The Vatican Library and Renaissance Culture* (Yale Univ. Press, the Library of Congress, and the Biblioteca Apostolica Vaticana, 1993).

Editor of Brahms Letters to Speak March 12

Styra Avins, editor and co-translator of the critically-praised first extensive edition of the letters of composer Johannes Brahms (1833-97), will speak on "Sleuthing Brahms" at a free brown-bag lunch Thursday, March 12, in Skillman Library's instruction room.

Avins, adjunct professor of music history at Drew University, Madison, NJ, studied cello and piano as a child, later studying at Juilliard School and the Manhattan School of Music, where she received her master's degree in cello.

She has been a member of the New York City Opera and American Symphony orchestras and served as principal cellist of the Seoul Symphony in Korea. She has also been active as a chamber instrumentalist and has performed all of Brahms' chamber and orchestral works.

"Sleuthing Brahms," Avins says, will focus on her efforts to track down information about the composer not found in the standard biographies and to locate throughout Europe and North America the 564 unpublished letters by Brahms that she selected, annotated, and translated with her husband, Josef Eisinger.

She will also discuss in a non-technical manner other kinds of new material in her edition of the letters, *Johannes Brahms: Life and Letters* (Oxford Univ. Press, 1997). The book has been praised by critic James B. Oestrich in the *New York Times* for its "bombshell" revisionist discovery that Brahms' did not, as had long been claimed, play piano as a youth in disreputable bars and brothels in the notorious St. Pauli section of Hamburg, his home. Biographers have long cited this alleged biographical detail to support Brahms' subsequent reputation, as Oestrich notes, as "aloof, misogynistic and often crude."

Throughout her volume, Avins provides useful biographical details, musical illustrations and chronological links for the letters. In particular, she raises questions about the alleged starvation of Robert Schumann (1810-56), composer friend of Brahms (and husband of Clara Schumann [1819-96], Brahms' longtime professional and personal colleague); instead, Avins cites evidence of Schumann's tertiary syphilis that led to his early death.

Avins and her husband live in Asbury, NJ.

Poet Sekou Sundiata's "Oralizing" to Help Open Desht Exhibit

by Elizabeth Sica

Photographer Martin Desht, whose works are exhibited this spring in Skillman's lobby and Special Collections Reading Room, was moved by a voice on the radio. Twice while driving to take photographs, once on North Broad Street in Philadelphia and again on 86th Street in Brooklyn, Desht listened to a velvety-smooth baritone recite poetry during two National Public Radio interviews. One line in particular, "Oh Harlem Oh Harlem Oh Harlem," echoed through his mind as he photographed the city street scenes.

The memorable voice belongs to performance poet Sekou Sundiata. Born and raised in Harlem, Sundiata's work is influenced by the music and oral traditions of African-American culture and follows in the footsteps of other notable street poets such as Amiri Baraka. His self-described "oralizing," rooted in the call-and-response dialogues of the black Baptist church, often marries his powerful vocal delivery with musical accompaniment.

Sundiata teaches at the New School for Social Research in New York City, and frequently takes his poetry on tour in Europe and the United States. In 1995 he was featured in the PBS special *The Language of Life* with Bill Moyers. A recent press release quotes Moyers describing Sundiata's work: "Sekou's music comes from so many places it is impossible to name them all. But I wager that if we could trace them to their common origin, we'd arrive at the headwaters of the soul."

A musician's sense of rhythm pulses through all of Sundiata's poems, even those he delivers a cappella. He explains: "Music is reference, source, resource, and inspiration to me as a writer and performer. In fact, it's damn near impossible to understand what contemporary black poets are doing without understanding what's going on with black music and its relationship to black speech and black literature."

The Blue Oneness of Dreams, Sundiata's debut album recently released on Mouth Almighty/Mercury Records, collects many of his works. Included on the CD is "Harlem, a Letter Home," the love poem to Harlem in its decline, whose longing refrain has stayed with Martin Desht. The poem begins: "It hurts me to my heart/ To see you like this/Underworld, Underweight/Impossible to be with/Impossible to leave...."

The Friends of Skillman Library are pleased to sponsor Sekou Sundiata's performance to help inaugurate the Desht photo exhibit. Scheduled for 7:30 p.m. on Tuesday, February 17 in Farinon Center's Marlo Room, the event is free and open to the public.

"*Poetry is this live thing, so there is always a process of revising and editing. Oftentimes I do poems that I don't feel are complete yet, but I can work them out on the bandstand. Whether I'm going to perform a poem or not, I always have to hear it out loud, over and over and over. My feeling for the poem is never satisfied on the page.*"

Sekou Sundiata, from an interview with Bill Moyers in *The Language of Life*

David Bishop Skillman Library

Exhibit
(continued from page 1)

the "Cape Cod, Poets, and Other Works" installation in the Special Collections Reading Room. On view here are some of Desht's first photographs, color images taken on board the Navy destroyer on which he worked in the early 1970s. Images of two widely different landscapes—Cape Cod and New York City—are part of this installation, as are portrait photographs of noted American poets—Philip Levine, Gerald Stern, Li-Young Lee, Len Roberts, and others. Desht's most recent project, an extension of the American Dream series into the inner-city of Philadelphia, is represented by photographs taken in and around Philadelphia's North Broad Street.

Opening events for the exhibit on February 17 include an afternoon reading by Martin Desht and reception (4:15 p.m., Skillman Instruction Room), and an evening performance by poet Sekou Sundiata (7:30 p.m., Marlo Room, Farinon Center). The exhibit will run from January 26 to July 31. The lobby exhibit can be seen during the hours the library is open, normally 8:30 a.m. to midnight; the reading room exhibit is available from 10 a.m. to 5 p.m. daily.

Woman and Child. North Broad and Oxford Streets, Philadelphia, Pennsylvania. From "Philadelphia: American City, American Dream." 1996.

Sea Grass. From "On Cape Cod." 1993.

Martin J. Desht, Photographer

Like the images he creates, Martin Desht's background reflects a remarkable range of experiences. The son and grandson of coal miners, he spent his early years in an orphanage. After high school in Allentown, he served as an engine room mechanic on board a U.S. Navy destroyer from 1968 to 1972 and as an industrial electrician at Bethlehem Steel from 1973 to 1978. At the steel mill, he repaired overhead cranes, a job with many moments of inactivity between operations. Desht filled the time with reading Faulkner, Fitzgerald, Salinger, and other American writers. It was during this period that he began to take college courses, first at Lehigh County Community College, then at Allentown College of St. Francis de Sales, from which he graduated in 1980 with a degree in English.

Laid-off by Bethlehem Steel in 1978, Desht bought his first real camera, an old Argus, for ten dollars from another unemployed steelworker. It was the beginning of a career that has included social documentary, fine art photography, and photo-journalism.

The 1989 collaboration with Lafayette history professor Richard Sharpless, "Faces from an American Dream," brought public attention and acclaim. The American Dream photographs have been exhibited at the U.S. Department of Labor, the Russell Rotunda of the U.S. Senate, the George Meany Memorial Archives, the American Labor Museum, New York University, Pennsylvania State University, and other venues. Desht has been the recipient of a number of grants and his photographs have been widely published.

Although the initial American Dream project is complete and Desht and Sharpless anticipate its publication in book form, Desht continues to document the consequences of the decline of industrial America. His latest project takes him into the streets of Philadelphia, a city once so heavily industrialized that it was known as the "workshop of the world." In neighborhoods where crime, drugs, and prostitution proliferate, he is once again capturing the face of civic and industrial abandonment.

Desht also passionately pursues his other photographic subjects—Cape Cod scenery, New York cityscapes, still lifes (especially of flowers), and poets; he is the unofficial photographer of the biennial Geraldine R. Dodge Poetry Festival in Waterloo Village, New Jersey. "Photography helps me search for truth," contends Desht. "I don't always find it, but it helps me search."

Industrial Welder and Daughter. Southeastern Pennsylvania. From "Faces from an American Dream." 1990.

High Tensions. Bethlehem Steel Corporation. Bethlehem, Pennsylvania. 1990.

Newsletters - 89

Ron Robbins

Assumes New Post

After 29 years as a familiar presence on the professional staff of Skillman Library, Ronald E. Robbins has assumed a new position at Lafayette College. Though Robbins' title and college office have changed—from head of public services in Skillman Library to assistant dean of studies in Markle Hall—his work and rapport with Lafayette students continues as he carries over skills developed over many years of working with Lafayette students in the library and in other activities such as women's cross-country and track.

Robbins came to Lafayette in 1968 as assistant reference librarian. Holder of three degrees—B.A. and M.A.T. in history, M.A. in library science—from Indiana University, Bloomington, Robbins became head reference librarian in 1970 and head of public services in 1990. In the latter position, he supervised circulation, reference, and inter-library loan staff, managed the library's physical facilities, and served as secretary of the Friends of Skillman Library in addition to overseeing student recruitment and train-

ing for the library.

"I'm confident," Robbins says, "that I can bridge the transition from library work to working with the dean of studies office, for both offices require similar skills in working with students."

Robbins' specific tasks in the dean of studies office include serving as dean for the sophomore and senior classes. He also coordinates on-campus classes during the January interim term, coordinates affiliated (non-Lafayette) study-abroad programs, arbitrates academic dishonesty cases, follows up on faculty referrals regarding students who are performing less than optimally, and deals with students with academic problems on a one-to-one basis or with the students' parents. (His colleague, associate dean of studies Sylvia R. Carey, serves as dean for the freshman and junior classes, coordinates peer counseling, works with students with disabilities, and coordinates minority student activities.)

In recent years, Robbins has also been active with the Northampton County Historical and Genealogical Society, serving as secretary to the board from 1993-95 and president from 1995-97; he presently serves as vice-president.

Dean of studies Christopher W. Gray says he is "delighted" that Robbins has joined his staff, for Robbins, Gray says, "knows both Lafayette and the personality of its faculty well, has a great deal of experience with student counseling, knows student strengths and failings, has heard all the usual student excuses for non-performance, and therefore knows how to be firm or to say 'no' when necessary, and he works well with the office's support staff." The position had been vacant for two years, since the death of

assistant dean of studies David M. Portlock, so Gray says he is especially pleased with Robbins' "immense contribution" to his office since he assumed the post last summer.

Robbins and his wife Bonnie, secretary to Lafayette's music and art departments, are parents of two daughters, one living in Boston, the other, with two children, in Virginia, where the entire family often gathers for get-togethers.

Clifford Stoll to Speak

Clifford Stoll, widely known as an astronomer, computer security expert, and critic of the computer revolution, will deliver this year's John and Muriel Landis lecture on Tuesday, March 10, at 8 p.m. in the Williams Center.

Stoll first came to public attention in March 1989 when the *New York Times* broke the story of his discovery and pursuit of a computer hacker. Stoll spent a year tracking the hacker through computer networks all over the world. The trail eventually led to a spy ring that sold computer secrets to the Soviet KGB. The story is related in Stoll's book *The Cuckoo's Egg: Tracking a Spy Through the Maze of Computer Espionage* (Doubleday, 1989).

Stoll's latest book, *Silicon Snake Oil: Second Thoughts on the Information Highway* (Doubleday, 1995), is a provocative discussion of the Internet and the way technology impacts our lives. Stoll was one of the first scientists to question some of the inflated claims made for the information highway. "The information highway is being sold to us as delivering information, but what it's really delivering is data . . . Unlike data, information has utility, timeliness, accuracy, a pedigree. Information, I can trust. But the data coming across America Online, or CompuServe or whatever, nobody stands behind it. Is the author a medical doctor or some bozo? I don't know . . . What's missing is anyone who will say hey, this is not good. Editors serve as barometers of quality, and most of an editor's time is spend saying no."

"I'm simply asking the questions out loud that most of my friends in computing have been talking about for the better part of a decade. My mom, who's pretty smart at age 75, said hey, this computer is hard to use. Nobody would listen to her. They listen to me. And I don't have any wisdom that my mother doesn't have."

Stoll's talk is open to the public without charge.

Welcome Back, Susanna

Two and a half years ago Skillman Library had the pleasure of hiring a bright, efficient, hardworking Interlibrary Loan Assistant. Her tenure with the library was brief as she received a scholarship to pursue her M.S.L.S. degree at Catholic University of America. In December of 1997, Susanna Boylston received that degree; on January 5, 1998, she returned to Skillman Library as our new Public Services Librarian.

A Bethlehem native, Boylston received her B.A. with honors in English literature from Sweet Briar College. She spent her junior year abroad studying at Oxford University, then returned to Oxford to earn a M.Litt. in English Literature.

While studying at Catholic University, she worked full time in the Interlibrary Loan and Circulation Departments as well as interned in the Reference Department. Boylston will use all of this experience in her new position at Lafayette where she will oversee circulation, stack maintenance, and the hiring and scheduling of student employees as well as serve as a reference and bibliographic instruction librarian. She is delighted to return to a library that she feels is committed to providing service of high quality. We are delighted to have her back, knowing from past experience how she will contribute to the services we offer.

IN MEMORIAM
HELEN STEVENSON MEYNER
1928-1997

Helen S. Meyner, former Congresswoman from New Jersey and wife of New Jersey Governor Robert B. Meyner '30, died in Fort Myers, Florida, on November 2, 1997. She leaves a lasting legacy at Lafayette in the Robert B. and Helen S. Meyner Center for the Study of State and Local Government, which she established in 1992, and in the collection of her personal and congressional papers in Skillman Library's Special Collections which were donated at the same time. In a memorial service held on campus on December 12, Lafayette president Arthur Rothkopf spoke about the legacy of the Meyner Papers:

This fascinating and important collection (which also includes materials related to Robert Meyner's life and career) captures what those who have worked most closely with the documents affectionately refer to as Helen Meyner's "spunk and spirit." Her inspiring sense of purpose; her unflagging energy; her resourcefulness; her irrepressible sense of fun; her commitment to the democratic process: these are but a few of the distinctive qualities that sing through her papers, whether she was writing as a young American Red Cross field worker during the Korean War, as the "First Lady" of New Jersey, or as a member of Congress.

David Bishop Skillman Library

1998 Spring Semester Programs

Tuesday, February 17
4:15 p.m. Talk by Martin Desht
5:00 p.m. Exhibit Opening and Reception
7:30 p.m. Performance by Sekou Sundiata

Tuesday, March 10
8:00 p.m. Landis Lectureship: Clifford Stoll

Thursday, March 12
Noon Brown Bag Talk: Styra Avins
"Sleuthing Brahms"

Thursday, April 30
5:30 p.m. Annual Reception and Dinner
8:00 p.m. Featured Speaker: Professor Anthony Grafton
"The History of Books and Reading"

CUR NON

Newsletter of the Friends of Skillman
Library, Lafayette College

The title "Cur Non" is taken from the coat
of arms of the Marquis de Lafayette and
means "Why Not?" Lafayette adopted this
motto shortly before sailing to America in
1777 to aid in the struggle for American
Independence. Published each spring and
fall at Lafayette College, Easton, PA 18042,
for members of the Friends of Skillman
Library and the Lafayette College community.

For information about membership in the
Friends of Skillman Library or about Friends'
programs, call 610-250-5150.

Neil J. McElroy, Director of Libraries and
  Academic Information Resources
Paul Schlueter, Editor
Susan Castelletti, Editorial Assistant

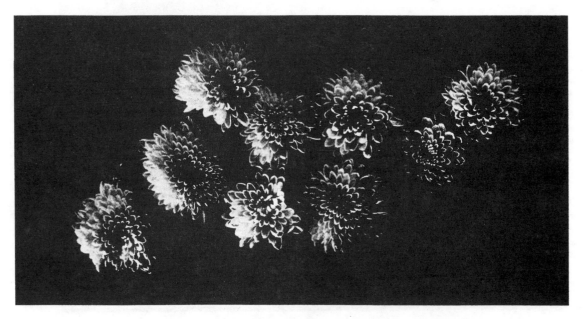

Mums. From "Greens Around the House." Martin J. Desht, 1993.

at the LIBRARY

Winter 1998

The Newsletter of the Friends of the Ohio Wesleyan Libraries

Celebrate Our Freedom

by Donald Lateiner

The historian observes that few societies in the past have enjoyed the freedoms that citizens of the United States possess to speak their minds, to read their books and journals, to see and to hear the arts that stimulate them, and to vote their consciences. Oddly, indeed paradoxically, such freedoms are both under-utilized by "we the people" and often reduced by lawyers and politicians to ill-defined, "hot button" issues of obscenity, pornography, and sacrilege. The noble word "adult" has been perverted in meaning to describe moving pictures and glossy photographs for those over eighteen whose minds reside in their private parts.

Often the "professionals" who determine what is protected or not by the Constitution have no training in relevant fields of intellectual and moral history. Many of the books and images that once were kept in locked cages in libraries, (if allowed into the country at all by the literary and moral critics employed by the United States Postal authorities), now are available to all, and wither sadly in a benignly neglected corner of our television-polluted cultural wasteland. Supreme Court Judge Potter Stewart's notorious 1964 quotation, "I shall not today attempt further to define [obscenity]...But I know it when I see it," encapsulates a disappointing inability to think about issues or, indeed, to admit that difficult thinking is required.

Aristophanes was brought before the Athenian People's Courts by his political foe Kleon for insulting

Donald Lateiner provides a dramatic reading from "Lysistrata" during the Banned Book Read-In.

that celebrated politician's policy and person. In the Rome of great Augustus, books of poets and historians were burned. In the Medieval and Renaissance periods, bodies were wracked and threats were freely uttered against those who had rediscovered a heliocentric universe or preached a different pathway to God. Whether or not the truth will make us free, certainly freedom does not always lead humans to truth. Too few people care. They do not care in part because there are too many colorful, "animated" diversions from the life of the mind or because they are too worn out by work and family to wrestle with great issues and great literature and great art.

continued on page 2

2.

Dare You Read This Book?

by Ruth Bauerle

Mark Twain's <u>Huckleberry</u> <u>Finn</u> is the most often challenged book of the 1990s, under repeated fire as "unsuitable" for high school English classes or school libraries. Its fault is Twain's use of the N-word "nigger," to refer to Huck's friend Jim. Most of us now find that offensive and cringe when we hear it. Yet it was the speech of the world Twain was writing about, and it would have been inconceivable for him to have Huck use a term like "Black" (which would have seemed even more of an affront in pre-Civil War Missouri) or "African-American." And a larger message of the novel is, after all, Huck's effort to help Jim escape slavery.

Huck's story is not the only book censored or challenged, however; it has the company, regrettably, of dozens of others every year, according to records of the Office of Intellectual Freedom of the American Library Association (ALA). Most challenges come not from a government office, but from members of the community, offended when a book clashes with their private standards of what is "appropriate" or "right."

To affirm our right to read and celebrate the First Amendment to the U.S. Constitution, Beeghly Library was host on September 23 to a five-hour read-in of banned or challenged books. On the front steps, despite a persistent drizzle and a chill northwest wind, thirty students, faculty, and townspeople read ten-minute segments of this "dangerous" literature. Each reader chose his or her own book from the listing provided by the ALA. Selections ranged

Dr. Tom Courtice reads from *Rabbit Run* during the Banned Book Read-In.

continued on page 9

Celebrate Our Freedom

continued from page 1

We celebrate a freedom from arbitrary suppression, from discriminatory sanctions against ideas that do not appeal to majorities. The disempowered by law enjoy a voice, if we protect that parchment wall against "know-nothing" or "know something" censors. Censorship of the controversial is political persecution. One person's blasphemy is another person's celebration of life. Let us continue to cultivate freedom of ideas, speech, and reading, as the event organized by Danielle Clark in the Library and retiree Ruth Bauerle invites us to.

The Bible, Sappho, Greek comedy, Roman epic, Boccaccio, Rabelais, Shakespeare, and countless other more recent explorers of the human condition have been censored. Censors live among us. They can be our neighbors and even friends. There are situations (in war, with young children, etc.) where censorship seems "natural" and right. But friends of liberty are constantly confronted with self-righteous men and women who think they know better than we what we ought to read or be permitted to contemplate. Juvenal asked "Quis custodiet ipsos custodes?," that is, roughly, "Who will censor the censors?" The freedom to read, to ponder and discuss what has been read, and to address issues of public concern is fundamental and necessary to a democracy and a republic.

Once the Bible in English was contraband. Once Americans rose against their government to demand freedom from censorship through stamp taxes on newspapers, books, etc. In our lifetimes, and now, people in the Soviet Union, in China, and in Iran (to name but a few) are thrown into jail (or worse) for writing and reading truths that make power uncomfortable. We owe it to them, to past fighters for freedom to read and write, and to ourselves to exercise our liberties. Let us use them or lose them.

Dr. Donald Lateiner is a professor of Humanities Classics.

Art Student Interns in Rare Books

by Hilda Wick

How nice to have friends in high places! Rare Books, a division of the Beeghly Archives, has a fortunate connection with the Art Department, and this relationship has resulted in challenging activities for senior art students and in valuable research and identification notebooks for Rare Books. Despite the name, Rare Books, this department has custody of what I often describe as all those things in the Library for which no one else wants the responsibility. There are pre-Colombian pots; Chinese gowns, scrolls, and tiles; African woodcarvings and masks; rare photographs; Oriental carpets; fragile chinaware; paintings; statues (busts); 4,000-year-old cuneiform tablets; and many other objects too numerous to mention. The need for organization of these artifacts, for descriptions of the physical objects, for identifications of source, origin and style, and for preservation is necessary if they are to be used or displayed intelligently. The art student interns provide enthusiastic aid and produce notebooks of great value to the Rare Books Department.

Senior art students who have taken or are taking art history courses, if identified by Dr. Carol Neuman de Vegvar, professor of Art History, as appropriate candidates for an art internship, are recommended to Hilda Wick, Rare Books Librarian, as suitable for an independent study or art internship in an area of the students's choice. The student's work is supervised by Dr. Neuman de Vegvar and, on site, by Hilda Wick.

In this article I would like to highlight the work of four interns whose work has enriched this department. The first student, Gina DeLuca, came to us in the fall of 1991, and her choice was the study of our American Indian pots, some of which are pre-Colombian, from the American Southwest and from the area of Bolivia near Lake Titicaca. She said in her summary of her work.

> During my first week in the Archives I was confronted with about 45 objects that I knew absolutely nothing about. Some looked very similar to others. Some looked very different. I needed to become familiar with these objects in order to begin research on them.

Obviously she did finally understand these pots because she organized the photographs and the pots; examined them closely; researched the shape, design, style, ornament, and origin; wrapped them in acid-free tissue for preservation; described and entered the research into the notebook. She searched books, articles, and museums for information and corresponded with archaeologists at the University of New Mexico, who aided greatly in the identifications and provided other information of value.

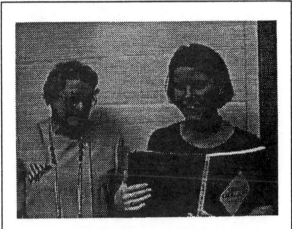

Art student intern Natalie Bailley holds the notebook she produced about Beeghly's American Indian Art.

We searched for the name of the donor of the Anasazi pots, but we were not successful in this endeavor. However, the donor of the Clow Collection, Jay L. Clow, '12, a missionary to the Aymara Indians of Bolivia, was known and some documentation was available: date of donation, donor, place of origin of the pots, etc. Other Clow artifacts such as clothing, fabrics, etc., were not included in this study. A splendid notebook with both black and white and colored photos was produced, pulling together all the information we could glean at that time, but with room for insertion of additional information as it becomes available. An extremely useful tool when we put our Indian artifacts on display, it also prevents extensive handling of the pots. These materials are fragile and largely unobtainable today, as governments are clamping down on the export of their cultural heritage.

Amy Tyler, the Spring 1992 intern, dealt with the rare photographs of Walt Whitman, a part of our famous Bayley-Whitman Collection of books, manuscripts, pamphlets, letters, ephemerae, and photographs. Walt Whitman must have been the most photographed American of the

continued on page 4

Art Student Interns
continued from page 3

19th century. Since there are over 300 photographs extant in American collections, he must have been very happy to pose over and over; the man who wrote "Song of Myself" should perhaps have written another one called "Photographs of Myself."

Amy sorted, labeled, identified the photographers and studios when the source is known, researched dates, names, photographic methods, inserted the photo or negative in plastic "sleeves" for preservation, and entered all our prints and negatives into a notebook which now contains over a hundred photos. This notebook is used very often as scholars from all over the United States request copies of our rare photos for displays at conferences or in new publications. To retrieve the proper photos, we have to identify the photos by code numbers familiar to all Whitman scholars, use the negatives to get a new print, or take the photo itself for digital reproduction at our favorite camera shop. Amy's notebook has saved uncounted hours of staff time; and best of all, it is a source than can be used by anyone to examine our holding of Whitman photos without handling the photos themselves.

In 1996, Beverly Smith, '97, was chosen as intern to organize the African artifacts collection. Her interest in non-Western art and her black heritage combined to make

Hilda Wick and Beverly Smith display one of the artifacts from the African Art Collection.

Beverly an extremely active and enthusiastic partner in research. She kept the Inter-Library Loan department busy for two semesters, and she visited other collections, talked with experts and a retired professor of African art, mounted a display of the objects, photographed them, and recorded

the vital statistics of some 40 objects: the provenance, the style, the use, the donor, and a summary of the historical background of the objects.

This notebook is stylistically professional and easily the most elegantly prepared. Her highly intelligent approach to the work and her computer skills, not to mention her deep appreciation of the objects, led her to take two semesters to finish the notebook, and I believe she enjoyed every minute of her extended research.

In the spring of 1997, Rare Books hummed with the activity and research of both Beverly Smith and Natalie Bailey, '97, who chose to examine, record, photograph, and do research on our antique Oriental carpets. Those who are not familiar with Oriental carpets will not realize the amount of knowledge necessary to understand the construction and colors, and to interpret the designs and motifs of these carpets. Even determining the origin can be a problem unless one studies the stylized figures and complicated designs, the number of "bands" or outer continuous designs, or perhaps the way the yarn is knotted.

Natalie studies the Middle Eastern areas involved in hand-woven carpet production, the history of carpet making, the dyes and yarns used, and the symbolic meaning of the elements of the design. Her photographs of the carpets, and especially her close-ups, are outstanding. A useful feature of the notebook is the many maps of Iran and Turkey on which one can find the towns where the weaving was done.

These well-motivated, hard-working students have given the Rare Books department useful notebooks; they have organized and researched interesting artifact collections; and we are proud of their dedication and their work. It is most enjoyable to work with these students as they eagerly pursue the knowledge they inevitably gain from such projects.

Hilda Wick is Rare Books and Special Collections Librarian.

Hugh B. Staples Gives Joyce Collection to Beeghly

by Ruth Bauerle

The gift to Beeghly Library of his private collection of books and periodicals on Irish writer James Joyce (1882-1941) was an act of extraordinary generosity by the late Hugh B. Staples, Ropes Professor of Comparative Literature at the University of Cincinnati. Dr. Staples (1922-1995) had been one of the early students of Joyce's work, beginning while he was still in the U.S. Army following World War II, and continuing until his death in Cincinnati in October, 1995.

Dr. Staples was important in the Joyce community as a contributor to journals and books on the great Irish writer and as a member of the editorial board of the respected James Joyce Quarterly. Often, too, he reviewed others' work in the Quarterly, so he became a shaper of Joyce scholarship in this century. His help is acknowledged in a number of important works of Joyce criticism, including Richard Ellmann's definitive biography, James Joyce; Adaline Glasheen's A Census of "Finnegans Wake"; and Louis Mink's A "Finnegans Wake" Gazetteer.

In addition to work on Joyce (now the second most cited author in English), Dr. Staples edited the diaries of Sir Jonah Barrington (a nineteenth century traveler in Ireland); wrote an early study of Robert Lowell's poetry (a work still being cited in Lowell scholarship); and did studies of poet Theodore Roethke and novelist Alan Sillitoe.

An October 8 reception welcomed the Staples Collection to Beeghly. Acting Director of Ohio Wesleyan Libraries Thomas Green pointed out the importance of such coherent collections to the growth of a college library and welcomed Dr. Staples' daughter, Elisabeth, and son, Hugh A. Staples. Ruth Bauerle, professor emerita of English at Ohio Wesleyan and a friend of Dr. Staples, spoke on "Singing at the Wake," developing the importance of music in James Joyce's life and writing. She was introduced by Dr. Joseph Musser, chair of the Department of English, which co-hosted the reception with Beeghly Library.

Items from the Staples Collection and posters from Ms. Bauerle's collection are on display in the Bayley Room. Particularly intriguing for a Joyce scholar is Dr. Staples' copy of Finnegans Wake. (Joyce deliberately omitted the apostrophe from that title, which refers not only to the Irish wake for the dead Tim Finnegan, but also, as noun-verb structure, to all Finnegans awakening at the resurrection.) Dr. Staples carefully annotated his Wake in the margins, so that his copy, which had been lovingly re-bound in leather, is a wonderful

Hugh A. and Elizabeth Staples stand in front of the James Joyce exhibit in the Bayley Room.

record of a fine scholar's study of the book.

Other interesting items in Dr. Staples' collection are a number of gift presentation copies, and a complete run of the rare and valuable periodical, A Wake Newslitter. (Again, "newslitter" is a Joycean coinage—apt, as his neologisms so often are.) There is a presentation copy of the Ellmann biography, as well as signed volumes from scholars David Hayman and Philip Herring, both at the University of Wisconsin; John Henry Raleigh, at Berkeley; and Mark Troy, in Sweden.

It is a typical Joycean coincidence that one of Dr. Staples' books is the Harvard doctoral dissertation of Marilyn French, The Book as World, a study of Joyce's greatest novel, Ulysses. (French was a fine Joyce scholar before she became a best-selling novelist.) This dissertation is displayed just below the stained glass window which portrays a book and a globe of the world, and the date 1904. Of course, 1904 is the year in which Ulysses takes place.

Beeghly is fortunate indeed to have this collection, which should be of significant value to students and teachers alike.

Ruth Bauerle is a retired member of the OWU English Department.

Think Chess

by Tom Green

Staunton-style chess pieces on a green and buff squared vinyl chess board sit on a table near the entrance of Beeghly Library. The set is in almost constant use by Ohio Wesleyan students. At the beginning of the 1996 academic year, Circulation Chief Bernard Derr put a chess set on the Beeghly Circulation Desk and, as time allowed, answered moves of all-comers over the course of the day. Soon the chess set moved from the Circulation Desk to the table where it is today. On Sunday afternoons student and community chess players of all ages gather in the second floor Bayley Room for friendly games of chess and instruction. What explains this interest in chess? Is playing chess an appropriate activity within the library?

Chess offers students the opportunity to compete in a sport that is based on intellect rather than physical prowess with the following benefits:

Improves the use of conceptual thinking;

Expands spatial thinking;

Develops decision-making abilities;

Stimulates the use of memory;

Encourages putting theory and ideas into practice;

Facilitates preparation and study;

Promotes sportsmanship;

Teaches critical thinking skills; and

Provides a lifetime of satisfaction and enjoyment.

The Bishops Chess Club formed during the 1990 spring semester when a dozen chess players met, wrote a constitution, and elected officers. Tom Wolber, assistant professor in Modern Foreign Languages, and I are co-advisors of the club. From the beginning, international students have assumed leadership roles in the chess club. Mansoor Jaffri, an Ohio Wesleyan student from Pakistan, was the first president. Other presidents include Krishna Tateneni, India; Ernesto Morejon, Venezuela; Brendan Kennedy, USA; Kahlid Salim, Germany; and the current president, Nosh Minwalla, Pakistan.

As stated in the constitution, the purpose of the chess club is "to develop an interest in the game among the general OWU student body" and to "give people a chance to play chess at a more organized and formal level." Chess club activities have evolved to meet these purposes. The Bishops Chess Club publishes a newsletter, plays a match with Kenyon College, and conducts chess tournaments. A student-only chess tournament is held annually and there are occasional special events such as a lecture and simultaneous exhibition by a Master chess player.

The club's first newsletter was published in October 1990. This four-page newsletter reported on tournament results, included five local games and chess news of interest to local players. In the following year the club started publishing two newsletters a year, one at the beginning of each semester. The most recent issue of *Bishops Chess Club News* is 18 pages in length with 93 games. The club also maintains a page on the World Wide Web at http://www.owu.edu/~tagreen/bishops.htm

In February, 1991, eight Ohio Wesleyan students traveled to Kenyon College for an inter-club match. Kenyon mustered six students for this first match. After accumulating a decisive 5-1 lead, Ohio Wesleyan students squandered several opportunities for wins or draws, allowing Kenyon to tie the match. Now chess players from the two schools meet twice a year, once at home and once away. Kenyon leads the series, but Ohio Wesleyan students always play competitively.

The first community-wide chess tournament was held in March, 1991. It attracted 16 chess players in an unrated event that awarded trophies as prizes. Alok Gyawali, a student from Nepal, was the clear winner with five wins. The first U. S. Chess Federation rated chess tournament was held in April, 1992. Two such tournaments are now held each year, the Trick or Treat Mini-Swiss around Halloween and the Ides of March Mini-Swiss at the end of Spring Break. In 1996 the tournaments moved to their current location in the Benes Room of the Hamilton Williams Campus Center. Last spring's event attracted 61 area chess players who played in seven sections.

The Bishops Chess Club and the Office of Student Activities co-sponsor a student-only chess tournament on Super Bowl Sunday. Twelve students participated in last year's event. After sharing first place honors the previous two years, Paul Milliman was undefeated in four rounds. Milliman, who graduated Phi Beta Kappa, typifies a student who achieved superior academic performance as well as high caliber chess. Probably the strongest student chess player to date was Alok Gyawali from Nepal. He made his U.S. tournament debut in the 1990 Columbus Open, where he won his first two games and drew a game against the eventual tournament winner. Alok finished with an Expert provisional rating of 2051. Kalpesh Asher, a freshman from Tanzania, joined the chess club this year with the distinction of a 3rd place finish in his country's national championship. His 6-2 record in that event included wins against the number one and two finishers.

Last year's officers expressed an interest in exploring the possibility of a statewide collegiate chess tournament. While events exist to determine the best players from kindergarten through high school, there is no collegiate event. Delaware's central location and the facilities of the Hamilton Williams Campus Center could provide an excellent venue, and the start of another tradition of the Bishops Chess Club.

In 1995 long-time Delaware chess player Jim Pool donated his chess book collection to Beeghly Library. This generous gift immediately created one of the better chess collections in any academic library in Ohio. No other OhioLINK libraries, for example, have the five-volume

Encyclopedia of Chess Openings or four volumes of *Encyclopedia of Chess Endings*. Other additions include Horowitz's *The Best in Chess* and *How to Think Ahead in Chess*, Chervev's *Most Instructive Games of Chess Ever Played*, and *Tal's 100 Best Games, 1961-1973*.

The Bishops Chess Club offers opportunities for Ohio Wesleyan students and Delaware area community members to grow in their knowledge and appreciation of chess. Beeghly Library is providing a unique environment for this development of chess culture.

Tom Green is the Acting Director of Libraries

Chess, anyone? Students take a study break in the Bashford Lounge.

Ohio Wesleyan Student Chess Champions:

1996-97: Paul Milliman
1995-96: Seng-Geap Goh and Paul Milliman
1994-95: Moy Easwaran and Paul Milliman
1993-94: T. J. Samuels
1992-93: Ernesto Morejon
1991-92: Ernesto Morejon
1990-91: Alok Gyawali

Congratulations

Congratulations to library Acquisitions Manager, Barbara Wiesner, who finished her coursework toward her Bachelor of Arts degree during the fall semester. Barbara is completing a double major in Women's Studies and Sociology/Anthropology. She was the recipient of the Emily Fitton Writing Award in the spring of 1997 for her paper about the Indians of North America. Her paper, entitled "As Long as the Grass Shall Grow: or The Long Road Through Hidden Agendas to Self Sovereignty," is housed in the OWU History/ Special Collections area of Beeghly Library. Barbara is expected to graduate Summa Cum Laude during commencement ceremonies on May 10, 1998.

At the Library

Edited by Ruth Davies, President of the Friends of the Ohio Wesleyan Libraries

Production Management by Bonnie Mahle, Library Administration Office Manager

Layout and Design by Jane Evans, Friends of the Library Volunteer

Special Thanks:
        to Audio Visual Manager Chuck Della Lana for his technical assistance with the graphics in this issue.

        to Christopher Yates and Mabi Ponce de Leon for providing courier service between Columbus and Delaware for the Newsletter during production.

OWU Book Discussion Group Begins Second Year!

by Danielle Clarke

Do you love to read? Do you love to talk about what you read? By answering these two questions, OWU community members formed the first OWU Book Discussion Group in the fall of 1996. Several students and two administrators constituted the charter membership. The group decided to meet 3-4 times each semester to discuss contemporary literature having a single theme. The fall, 1996, theme was "Love and Loss." Using the rhyme "Something old, something new, something borrowed, something blue," the group read Edith Wharton's Ethan Frome ('old'), Josephine Hart's Damage (new), Heinrich Boll's The Lost Honor of Katharina Blum ('borrowed' — translated from the German), and Marguerite Duras' The Lover ('blue' - prize-winning title). In spring semester 1997, the group concentrated on life stories of adolescent women who faced hardships with resolve, resiliency, and spunk. The books were I Know Why the Caged Bird Sings by Maya Angelou, Rubyfruit Jungle by Rita Mae Brown, Ellen Foster by Kaye Gibbons, and The Liars' Club by Mary Karr. In spite of rape, incest, alcoholism, abandonment, abuse both physical and mental, the young women in these stories inspired enthusiastic discussions about the power of spirit.

With a new member the group began meeting for fall semester 1997 to discuss four books about life in the Caribbean Islands for young women. The theme was "Mangoes, Machetes, and Memories." The books are written by four exciting and well-reviewed young women authors who are from four different islands in the Caribbean Sea. The group read Julia Alvarez' How the Garcia Girls Lost Their Accent (Dominican Republic), Esmeralda Santiago's When I Was Puerto Rican (Puerto Rico), Cristina Garcia's Dreaming in Cuban (Cuba), and Edwidge Danticat's Breath, Eyes, Memory (Haiti). Because all of these young authors are relatively newcomers to contemporary fiction, here are some brief descriptions of their works and biographical sketches of their island and immigrant experiences.

Julia Alvarez was actually born in New York; however, she was reared on the island of her family (Dominican Republic) until she was ten years old. Her work, How the Garcia Girls Lost Their Accent, is the fictional account of four sisters who were reared in The Dominican Republic until the family was exiled. The book is arranged in an unusual time chronology: part one (1982-1972) is actually the "current time" or the present to the four sisters who each

"write" chapters; part two is the most recent past (1970-1960) and describes the period of adjusting to New York City and learning to live without the support of an extended family and financial comfort; part three reflects the earliest childhood memories of the four daughters in their idyllic memories of island life. Donna Rifkind, a reviewer for the New York Times Book Review, remarked that the idea of a "reverse chronology" was "a shrewd idea" and that Alvarez "has...beautifully captured the threshold experiences of the new immigrant, where the past is not yet a memory and the future remains an anxious dream." (10/6/91, p.14)

Esmeralda Santiago was born in Puerto Rico as the eldest of 11 children who lived in rural poverty outside San Juan; she attended the High School for Performing Arts in New York City and went on to Harvard. Her memoir, When I Was Puerto Rican, describes both the joys and uncertainties of living with parents who love and hate each other. When Esmeralda was 13, her mother moved her children to Brooklyn in search of a better life. There was joy in the Brooklyn Public Library where it was quiet and filled with wonderful books (all in English) and always a place to sit. In a Library Journal review Gwen Gregory states: "While she shares unique personal experiences, Santiago also expresses the universality of growing up. ... Santiago's story reflects that of Puerto Rico: to be a part of the United States, yet distinct and somehow detached." This beautifully written story reveals a young woman who decided to meet the challenges of a new country with enthusiasm.

Cristina Garcia's first novel, Dreaming in Cuban, is the story of Celia, a pro-Castro revolutionary grandmother, her exiled husband, their daughters, Lourdes, who runs a bakery in Miami, and Felicia, who suffers the agonies of syphilis in Cuba. There is a son, Javier, and many grandchildren both in Cuba and Miami, who feel torn between the two worlds of their family, divided by politics, distance, misunderstandings, and longing. Thulani Davis says in the New York Times Book Review: "Like Louise Erdrich, whose crystalline language is distilled of images new to our American literature but old to this land, Ms. Garcia has distilled a new tongue from scraps salvaged through upheaval."

Edwidge Danticat spins the story of four generations of women as they experience poverty, violence, and prejudice in the Haiti and the United States in her first novel,

Breath, Eyes, Memory. Danticat was born in Haiti; her parents emigrated to the US when she was four. For nine years she lived with an aunt in Haiti until she joined her parents at the age of 13. Margaria Fichtner says that Danticat's writing "has much to say about what it is like to be young, black, Haitian and female wandering in a world too often eager to regard all of those conditions as less than worthwhile."

The themes of growing up between to worlds is best described by Cristina Garcia in an article: "Those of us who straddle two cultures are in a unique position to tell our stories, share our vision, imagination, history. Far more often, we're bilingual—and bicultural—than were previous generations. Our presence does not require anyone's blessing. ...I realize I do belong in two places. Two cultures coexist within me, if not always equally, then companionably."

The OWU Book Discussion Group meets in the Kleist Conference Room on the Main Floor of Beeghly Library.

If you would like to join the book discussion group, please call Danielle Clarke (368-3237) at Beeghly Library, or E-mail: mdclarke@cc.owu.edu.

Danielle Clarke is a Public Services Librarian

Book Discussion Group
Spring 1998 Schedule

February 10: Song of Solomon by Toni Morrison

March 3: The Old Man and the Sea by Ernest Hemingway

April 14: Animal Dreams by Barbara Kingsolver

Dare You Read This Book?
continued from page 2

historically from Aristophanes' Lysistrata to Peter Wright's Spycatcher, and thematically from the Bible to "The Three Billy Goats Gruff." Reasons for challenging these and other books included frankness about sexuality (which some persons dispute in the Bible itself), violence in a story (those goats did beat up the troll!), language someone found "objectionable," revelations about military intelligence, the Jewish birth of a Catholic composer, the anti-war impact of a play, and language perceived as "racist." Maya Angelou's account of her brutal rape when she was a small child (in I Know Why the Caged Bird Sings) was banned in one community as "pornographic."

President Thomas Courtice led off at 10 a.m. reading from Updike's Rabbit Run; professors Lynette Carpenter, Kaaren Courtney, Margaret Fete, Robert Flanagan, John Gatz, Bonnie Milne Gardner, Robert Gitter, Michael Grote, Martin Hipsky, Paul Kostyu, Donald Lateiner, Corinne Lyman, Cheryl McGinnis, and Thomas Wolber were joined by Acting Director of OWU Libraries Thomas Green. Prof. Marilyn Nims sang a song from Gustav Mahler. Student readers included Nikki Reiss, Colin Frost, Abby Howard, Bernadette Dethier, Andrea Misko (who also edits The Transcript) and Cameron Hewitt. Delaware community readers included Gazette reporter Jesse Carter, Rev. Thomas van Brunt and Rev. Warren Campbell-Gaston of St. Peter's and Asbury churches, city attorney and OWU trustee Daniel Bennington, Common Pleas Judge Henry Shaw, and media free-lancer Sherry Sheets, whose three year old daughter interjected "Gruffff!" at appropriate points as her mother read the fairy tale. Elizabeth Barker and Patricia Ebbatson, directors of the Ashley and Delaware County public libraries, and M. Edward Hunter, librarian emeritus at Methesco, were supportive readers. Co-chairs for the event were M. Danielle Clarke, Public Services Librarian at Beeghly, and Ruth Bauerle, professor emerita of English, both of whom also read.

Only one complaint about the event has reached Beeghly—from those who wondered why they hadn't been given an opportunity to take part. Planners tried to represent every department and discipline on campus, and had stretched the time an extra hour to include volunteers. There is talk, however, of "next time," and perhaps this will become a regular Beeghly event.

Ruth Bauerle is a retired member of the OWU English Department

New Staff Members at Beeghly Library

by Tom Green

Marsha Zavar is our new Interlibrary Loan/Public Services Office Manager. She has an M.L.S. degree from Kent State University and a B.A. from Youngstown State University. Marsha came to us from the Upper Arlington Public Library where she was a Librarian Assistant. She replaces Sarah Bergman who resigned in January.

Christopher Yates is our new Assistant Chief of Circulation. He is nearing the completion of a master's degree in library science from Kent State. He has a B.F.A. degree from Columbus College of Art and Design and an

M.F.A. degree from the State University of New York at Stony Brook. He is a practicing artist whose work has been selected for many exhibitions and he writes reviews for *Dialogue: Arts in the Midwest*. Chris replaces Cynthia Short who resigned in June to accept a position as Chief of Circulation at Capital University.

Terry Maloney-Rose was hired for a temporary, part-time assignment coordinating collection development, including gifts and exchanges, and managing the government publications collection. Terry has her M.L.S. from Kent

State University, a B.A. in Art History from Boston University, and an M.A. in Art History from Michigan State University. Last spring, Terry provided Interlibrary Loan services on an interim basis.

Carol Holliger was hired for a temporary, part-time position as a Reference Librarian. Carol has her M.L.S. from Kent State University, a B.A. in Sociology from Whitman College, and an M.A.R. from Yale Divinity School. Her most recent library experience was at the University of Akron Wayne College Library in Orrville, Ohio. Carol works at the Beeghly Reference desk Monday evenings and Tuesday through Friday afternoons. Terry and Carol are providing much needed services until the University decides how to fill the positions vacated by Kathleen List, Director of Libraries, and Sha Li Zhang, Head of Technical Services.

Holiday Thanks for Student Assistants

Twice a year, right before finals week, library staff members get together for what is affectionately referred to as "goodie bag stuffing". Goodie bags have become a tradition at the library. Staff escape, for a few minutes, from their busy desks and gather in the staff lounge. Goodie bags, one for each student assistant, are filled with staff donations of candy, cookies and other assorted yummies. This is a fun and tasty way to show our student assistants how much we appreciate all they do for us.

Library Staff Receives CPR Certification

Linda Strapp instructs library staff members on lifesaving skills during the November CPR training class.

Twelve library employees attended a November 6 class in Cardio-Pulmonary Resuscitation and received Red Cross certification. Linda Strapp, an Ohio Wesleyan University physical education instructor, taught the CPR course. Though we hope we never need to use our training, we feel it is important, as members of a public service institution, to be prepared for any emergency situation.

Here's to Ruth!

by Bonnie Mahle

Ruth Davies was fifteen years old when she arrived on the Ohio Wesleyan campus in 1923. When Ruth graduated from Ohio Wesleyan, she did so with the best academic record in the history of the University. Halfway through her first year of graduate school at the University of Chicago, Ruth received a letter from Ohio Wesleyan asking her to come back to teach. Her reply was "No thanks. I have other plans." A second letter, doubling the salary offer, succeeded in bringing her back, "but only for one year." The rest, as they say, is history. That one year commitment has stretched into a 75-year odyssey.

Although Dr. Davies officially "retired" in 1973, she continued teaching part-time through 1986. This tied the record for fifty-seven consecutive years teaching previously set by William G. Williams. If we add those years teaching to the years she was a student, we realize that Ruth Davies has been an integral part of Ohio Wesleyan University for nearly half of its history. In a very real sense, the history of Ohio Wesleyan lies in Ruth Davies' memory, and chronicled in her records.

To this day, Ruth Davies remains active within the university community. This year marks the tenth anniversary of the Friends of the University Libraries that she founded in 1987. As President of the Friends, Ruth continues recruiting new members, encourages continuing support of current

Friends of the OWU Libraries President, Ruth Davies.

Photo courtesy of Mrs. Howard Shearer

members, and is the editor of "At The Library," the Friends' semi-annual newsletter.

Ruth Davies celebrated her ninetieth birthday in October. Several gatherings, including one at Austin Manor, hosted by friends Ruth Melvin, Mary Bossert, and Helen Taggart, marked the occasion. The legacy Ruth Davies has provided Ohio Wesleyan during the years continues to grow, enriching the entire university community.

Bonnie Mahle is library liaison to the Friends of the OWU Libraries

New and Renewing Members

Name _____

Address _____

_____

Individual Memberships   Family Memberships

☐ 1 Year $15 (December '97 - December '98)   ☐ 1 Year $15 (December '97 - December '98)

☐ 2 Years $30 (December '97 - December '99)   ☐ 2 Years $30 (December '97 - December '99)

Send to:
Dr. Ruth Davies
Beeghly Library
Ohio Wesleyan University
Delaware, Ohio 43015

Friends

A New Year Greeting from the Kate Greenaway Collection, housed in the Special Collections of Beeghly Library.

U.S. Postage
PAID
BULK RATE
PERMIT 23
Delaware, Ohio
Non-Profit Org.

Friends of the Ohio Wesleyan Libraries
Delaware, Ohio 43015

Jessie Ball duPont Library

FRIENDS OF THE LIBRARY
University of the South
founded 1982

Newsletter No. 26   Spring 1997

Editor, Phoebe S. Bates

SPRING MEETING. Our next meeting will be at 4 P.M. on Friday, April 25, in the Torian Room. Our speaker will be Dr. William T. Cocke III, Jesse Spalding Professor of English at the College, yclept "Willie," who will give a talk on his lifelong scholarly interest, entitled "Shakespeare's Indispensable Book." Dr. Cocke graduated from the University of the South in 1950 and later received his Ph.D. from Vanderbilt. He loves Sewanee and has taught here for thirty years—a distinguished career as teacher, scholar, friend, respected colleague. His circle of friends is immense, and he is much in demand as a speaker and representative of the University among alums across the country.

At the spring meeting we will also elect new officers and members of the board. A nominating committee, composed of Charles DuBois, Corrie Norman, and Tom Watson, will present a slate. In addition to local nominees, they also are looking for out-of-town board members (we feel we need to enlarge our scope), so if you have good suggestions, please speak to one of these people.

Finally, we are considering having more frequent meetings of the Friends of the Library. Tentatively, we would like to consider at least an annual program or conference on subjects such as Sewanee authors. We also would like to think about some small field trips, perhaps to see the Flannery O'Connor materials in Milledgeville, or to attend the annual Conference on Southern Literature in Chattanooga. Please let us have your suggestions about such things.

—John Paul Carter, President

FORECAST OF THINGS TO COME. Our fall 1997 speaker, on December 4, will be Dr. Charles T. Cullen, President and Librarian of the Newberry Library, Chicago, one of the major resource and research centers in the United States. Dr. Cullen graduated from Sewanee in 1962 and received an M.A. from Florida State and Ph.D. from the University of Virginia. The University of the South awarded him a D.Litt. in 1994. An expert on American legal history in the 18th and 19th centuries, he edited the papers of Thomas Jefferson and the papers of John Marshall. In addition, he has written many scholarly papers and is much sought after as a speaker. His talk will deal with the Newberry Library and the special role of research libraries.

HOUSEKEEPING TIPS. If you will rearrange your book shelves, you might find extra room for the bargains which you will find at the annual spring book sale at duPont on Wednesday, April 23 (details to be announced). There will be an advance sale period reserved for members of the Friends of the Library. On sale will be duplicates of books already in the collection or ones which are being discarded. Just another advantage to being a member of the Friends!

THE FUTURE OF BOOKS Whenever I am with a group of people, attending a social function on or off campus, I am inevitably asked, "Is the library still buying books?" The question is always asked in a joking manner, but the asker's voice also always betrays just a bit of apprehension that I might actually respond in the negative. Those who, like most of the readers of this newsletter, love books, both as conveyors of wisdom and good literature and as valuable and interesting artifacts of our civilization, are understandably discomfited by those who are predicting that the electronic revolution inevitably seals the doom of the printed word on paper. We have all read articles in the popular press predicting that by some specified date, usually early in the twenty-first century, books will have become as scarce as illuminated manuscripts became after the emergence of the printing press in the fifteenth century.

These same futurologists further predict that one major consequence of the disappearance of books will be the disappearance of librarians and the profession of librarianship, since they erroneously assume that librarians are primarily the custodians of collections of books, a model which has not characterized librarianship for at least three decades now. Custodianship of the library's books has never constituted more than a minor part of librarians' responsibilities, except perhaps in the earliest period of the emergence of librarianship as a profession. The primary responsibility of librarians throughout the greater part of the twentieth century has been the organizing and the interpreting of information resources for library users. The emergence of digital information resources, especially the explosion of information on the World Wide Web has only increased the value which librarians bring to the table. No other profession has the training and expertise to cope with this overwhelming proliferation of electronic information resources.

In the working academic or research library, only two major areas have been significantly affected thus far by digital information resources, the reference area and the periodicals area. The reasons are fairly obvious. Many standard reference works are cumbersome to use effectively, but their electronic counterparts are much more powerful in their searching capability and thus provide users with additional and more effective ways to access the information contained in them; in short, they tend to provide the user much more for the library dollar spent. The explosion of digitized journals, on the other hand, is being driven primarily by economics. No library today, even the most liberally funded and generously endowed, can afford to own more than a fraction of the journal titles needed by its readers. We are beginning to see academic libraries like duPont replacing growing numbers of their paper subscriptions and back files with on-line and CD-ROM versions.

DuPont Library, however, like most other academic libraries, continues to experience annual increases in its library materials budget. For example, duPont's materials budget has increased an average of 5% for each of the past five years, and I expect to see such growth in traditional library materials continue indefinitely. Most library users expect to find the materials they want to read for leisure or for general intellectual enlightenment in traditional book format. I seriously doubt that this will change any time soon, if ever.

Yet clearly, in today's libraries as in tomorrow's, both types of resources have their place and play their own appropriate roles in meeting users' varied information, enrichment, and leisure needs.

—Tom Watson, University Librarian

STAFF NEWS. Eloise Ramsey Hitchcock is a new face on duPont's first floor, as she has assumed the position of Head of Reference. Young as she looks—and is—Mrs. Hitchcock has had considerable library experience before landing in Sewanee. She was first at Tennessee Tech in Cookeville, where she received her B.S. in history *cum laude*, and then at UT-Knoxville, where she took her master's in library science. Subsequently, she held positions at Berea College, MTSU, and again Cookeville before coming to Sewanee. Each new job entailed new skills learned, so that the reference department is very pleased with her appointment, as are the library users.

Mary O'Neill is the coauthor with former duPont librarian John Spencer of a bio-bibliographical article on Allan Gurganus, North Carolina-born novelist and author of *The Oldest Living Confederate Widow*, which appears in the March 1997 *Bulletin of Bibliography*.

New in circulation is Sarah Briggs, a graduate of Washington and Lee, who is working on a master's degree at Vanderbilt Divinity School. Her previous library experience was at the Vanderbilt Divinity Library.

THE FRIENDS OF THE LIBRARY FUND has been initiated by a recent gift of $500. President Jack Carter hopes to develop the Fund as a significant endowment for the library, both to assist its ongoing mission and to provide extra-budget funding for special needs. Friends of the Library are urged to contribute and feel free to solicit like-minded friends.

THANKS are extended to the following for gifts to purchase library materials: Dr. & Mrs. Fred Allison, Jr., Dr. & Mrs. Scott Bates, the Church of the Resurrection (Starkville, MS), Ms. Ruth Duperret, Dr. Sherwood Ebey, Mr. & Mrs. Oscar P. Fitzgerald, Jr., Mr. & Mrs. Oscar P. Fitzgerald IV, Mr. and Mrs. Richard Fitzgerald, Dr. John Flynn, the Fortnightly Club, Mr. Bradford Gioia, Mr. Eugene Ham, Mr. & Mrs. J. Samuel Hammond, Ms. Gloria Harris, Dr. & Mrs. Robert Keele, Mr. Joe David McBee, Mr. & Mrs. Arnold Mignery, Ms. Leila Parmee, Mr. Samuel W. Preston III, Dr. & Mrs. John Reishman, Dr. Harris D. Riley, Jr., Sewanee Arts and Crafts, Ms. Carolyn Stewart, Vulcan Materials Co., Mr. Jerome Wagner, and Dr. Herbert Wentz.

For books and other library materials the library thanks Dr. Laurence Alvarez, the Annenberg Washington Program, Ms. Anne Armour-Jones, Mr. Laurie Atkinson, Mr. Harold Baldridge, the Bibliographical Society of the University of Virginia, Mr. Dan Binder, Mr. Sam Boyd, the Rev. William Brettman, Mr. Beeler Brush, Mrs. T.E. Butt, the Consulate General of Israel in Atlanta, Ms. Penny Cowan, Crossroad Publishing, Dr. Joseph Cushman,

Thanks also to Mrs. Chauncey W. Durden, Jr., Dr. Doug Durig, *Earth and You*, the Ford Foundation, Mr. Jim Fulbright, Dr. Harold Goldberg, Dr. Anita Goodstein, Mr. Rich Gosling, Mr. Marlan Green, Mr. Edwin Greninger, Dr. John Hamer, Jacksonville State University, Ms. Linda Jones, Ms. Cecilia Kelly, Mr. F.J. Kelly,

Mr. William Kershner, Sister Kiara CSM, Mr. and Mrs. Louis Koella, Mr. John Kolyer, Mr. Blucher Lines, S. J. Magyarody, Ms. Margaret Martin, Mr. Laurence Masters, Mr. Charles Matt, Mr. Greg Maynard, Mr. Belden Menkus, Mr. & Mrs. Mills Morrison, Dr. Eric Naylor, Olin Gallery at Kenyon College, Dr. Brown Patterson, Dr. Diane Petrilla, Dr. George Poe, Dr. Stephen Puckette, Mr. John Ransom, Mr. Alfred Richardson, Ms. Judy Rickman, Dr. Cären Rosser, Mr. John Shackelford, Dr. Gerald Smith, Mr. Jerome Spevack, Mr. John Sullivan, Mr. & Mrs. Frank Thomas, University Gallery, Mr. Robert Van Dyke, Prof. Merle Wallace, Dr. Samuel Williamson, Mr. & Mrs. Robert Wickham, and the World Bank.

Please join THE FRIENDS OF THE LIBRARY. Fill in and mail the form below to: The Friends of the Library, The University of the South, 735 University Avenue, Sewanee, Tennessee 37383-1000.

NAME _____

ADDRESS _____

TELEPHONE (Area Code) _____ (Number) _____

MEMBERSHIP DESIRED: _____ Student ($5) _____ Family ($25)

_____ Single ($15) _____ Patron ($50 & up)

Newsletter of the Friends of the Library
The University of the South
735 University Avenue
Sewanee, TN 37383-1000

LIBRARY PERSPECTIVES

A Newsletter of the Oberlin College Library

NUMBER EIGHTEEN   FEBRUARY 1998

Information Literacy Workshops

The Library held two information literacy workshops for faculty during the month of January — one for the faculty as a whole and another designed specifically for the Politics Department. The workshops represent a continuation of efforts begun last year, following the General Faculty Library Committee's report on information literacy, which documented the need to improve the library research skills of Oberlin students. The workshops were developed with the twin goals of acquainting faculty more fully with new information technologies and discussing with them possible ways of increasing the integration of information literacy skills into the curriculum.

Over forty faculty members from a variety of departments participated in a five-session workshop on "Using Educational Technology to Teach Information Literacy." Taught jointly by staff of the Library and the Oberlin Center for Technologically Enhanced Teaching (OCTET), the workshop followed up on many of the topics of the Library's first faculty information literacy workshop in January 1997 (*Library Perspectives*, February 1997). Sessions taught *continued page 7*

Scenes from the Library/OCTET Workshop

Lexis-Nexis Now Available on the Web

The Oberlin College Library recently became a subscriber to Lexis®-Nexis® UNIVerse, a user-friendly Web-based version of Lexis-Nexis, a comprehensive online source of news, legal, and business information.

The information sources included in Lexis-Nexis UNIVerse were compiled specifically for the needs of academic institutions. Lexis-Nexis UNIVerse couples the convenience of the Internet with the power of Lexis-Nexis services to quickly and easily retrieve documents that meet specific research needs. To search Lexis-Nexis UNIVerse the user simply selects from a list of research categories and completes an electronic search form.

Lexis-Nexis offers news from more than 7,000 English-language newspapers, newsletters, magazines, trade journals, wire services, and broadcast transcripts, including the Associated Press, *The New York Times,* and CNN.

Additionally, Lexis-Nexis offers premier news sources in the French, Italian and German languages as well as comprehensive, current legal information, including federal and state case law, statutes, and secondary sources such as law reviews, state legal materials, and directories. Such commonly used reference tools as *Books in Print, Encyclopedia of Associations,* and *Ulrich's International Periodicals Directory* are included as well.

Professor of Sociology James Walsh notes that "Keeping up with *continued page 6*

Friends Meeting Highlights

The Friends of the Library held its annual meeting on Saturday, November 1. The group heard a report from the membership committee and discussed ways to increase membership; voted to increase the basic and couples membership to $30 and $40 respectively; discussed ways in which the Friends might raise additional funds for the Library; heard a report from the program committee as well as a report on a potential symposium for alumni librarians; and discussed the progress of the Student Friends of the Library.

The Friends Council authorized purchases for the Library collections totaling $15,334, as recommended by the Acquisitions Committee (see related article this page). The membership also elected new council members and officers for the 1998-99 year.

Minutes of the meeting are available on the Friends website (http://www.oberlin.edu/~library/friends/friends.html) and by request from:

Friends of the
    Oberlin College Library
Mudd Center
Oberlin College
Oberlin OH 44074-1532

Purchases with Friend Funds

The Friends of the Library Council authorized the use of over $15,000 of funds contributed to the Friends to acquire a variety of materials for the Library. The funds will assist the Library in building general collections that support selected new curricular areas as well as areas that require further development. They will also be used to purchase three major reference works, four microfilm research collections, and a facsimile manuscript for special collections.

The following is a summary by category of these most recent Friends purchases:

Materials for New Curricular Areas ($4,000)

1. Asian American Studies. The emerging curriculum in Asian American Studies continues to expand. New courses are being offered in Asian American Labor History, Asian American Religious History, and in the Asia Pacific American Experience. These funds will provide basic collection support for these courses.

2. Native American Studies. Funds will provide collection support for new courses in Native American Studies that have recently been added to the curriculum.

Italian Language and Literature ($1,000)

These funds will be used to continue filling gaps in holdings of twentieth-century Italian language and literature in support of the work of Professor Davida Gavioli.

Major New Reference Works ($3,990)

1. *Routledge Encyclopedia of Philosophy* (10 vols., Routledge, 1998). This new, standard reference work in philosophy has been requested as a top priority by the Philosophy Department. The Library will acquire both the CD-ROM and printed versions of the encyclopedia, which are available as a package.

2. *Index Kewensis* (CD-ROM for Windows, Oxford University Press, 1997). This index is "the world's most comprehensive registry of plant names," containing information on species, family, genus, and references to the literature where the plant was first described. It began publication in 1893, with 19 supplements to 1996.

3. *Microscopic Anatomy of Invertebrates*, ed. by Frederick W. Harrison (vols. 6,13,15, Wiley-Liss, 1991-). These volumes will complete the Library's holdings for this essential work in anatomy.

Primary Source Materials to Support Teaching and Research ($4,038)

1. *History of Women Collection*. (Microfilm of Unit 20: Pam-
continued page 5

In Appreciation of the Friends

Remarks by Oberlin College President Nancy Dye at the Friends Dinner, November 1, 1997

I am pleased to have the chance to make a few remarks tonight to the Friends of the Oberlin Library. This is my fourth year at the College, and I count our Friends of the Library dinners among our most interesting and enjoyable occasions. Johnetta Cole's speech in 1994 and Margaret Atwood's appearance last year were especially memorable. Judging from Tony Grafton's fascinating lecture this afternoon, tonight's talk will continue in the same tradition.

I want to take this opportunity to pay tribute to the generous support provided to our library by the Friends. With the assistance of Friends' funds, our library has been able to acquire special materials which in all likelihood could not have been purchased otherwise. Over just a few years, the Friends have contributed more than $100,000 to special library acquisitions. I know that faculty are especially grateful for the support

Nancy Dye

of new courses and programs which this funding has made possible.

Oberlin has a great library. It is outstanding in the depth of its collections. It is outstanding in the ways in which library materials of all sorts are increasingly available to the College community. It is outstanding for the remarkable friendliness and accessibility of our library to all of our students. And it is outstanding in the ways in *continued page 6*

Grafton Talk Available

Anthony Grafton, Dodge Professor of History at Princeton University, delivered an entertaining and infomative slide talk at the Friends of the Library annual dinner on November 1 about ways in

Anthony Grafton

which historians study the history of reading. The talk is now available in video format (see below).

Professor Grafton started his talk by saying "I'd like to take you tonight into a lost world of the study as you lived in it as a Renaissance reader — it's a magnificent world." He went on to discuss ways in which historians today are able to piece together a history of reading in the Renaissance using evidence such as commentaries and annotations in books from the time, and the reconstruction of the libraries of various individuals from the 15th and 16th centuries.

Professor Grafton pointed out some of the more remarkable dif- *continued page 7*

Friends Honor Life Members

The Friends of the Library awarded life memberships to three couples at the annual Friends dinner on November 1.

William Perlik, chairman of the Oberlin College Board of Trustees, announced the awards and expressed appreciation on behalf of the Friends and the College for the generous support given the Library by each of the recipients:

Geraldine and Richard Meyer of River Forest, Illinois. Mrs. Meyer, a member of the Oberlin class of 1942, has served on the Library Visiting Committee since its inception in 1990 and also as a member of the Library mini-campaign steering committee. Mr. and Mrs. Meyer have been exceptionally generous in making gifts to both the Friends of the Library and to the Library mini-campaign.

Bruce Regal and Theresa Brown of New York City. Mr. Regal and Ms. Brown are both members of the Oberlin class of 1978. Ms. Brown served on the Library mini-campaign steering committee. She and Mr. Regal have been generous contributors to the library acquisitions endowment, the library special book fund, and especially to the library mini-campaign. Their contributions to the latter will be applied to the construction of a new science library, which is being planned as part of a major college project to upgrade the science facilities at Oberlin.

Lloyd and Beatrice Frank of New York City. Mr. Frank, Oberlin Class of 1947, has served on the Library Visiting Committee. He and Mrs. Frank have made generous contributions to the library special book fund, to the Friends of the Library, and to the Library mini-campaign.

Alumni Librarian Symposium

The Friends of the Library Council gave tentative approval at its meeting on November 1, 1997 to the idea of a symposium for Oberlin alumni who work in libraries. Current plans call for holding the symposium during the fall of 1999, on the same weekend as the Friends of the Library dinner.

The idea of the symposium was first discussed at the 1996 Friends Council meeting when Friends Secretary Mike Haverstock noted how frequently he was in correspondence with alumni who are librarians. Haverstock suggested that it might be worthwhile to investigate the feasibility of a symposium or conference of Oberlin alumni librarians, focusing perhaps on the library of the future.

Molly Horst Raphael '67, Acting Director of the District of Columbia Public Library, and Ray English, Director of Libraries at Oberlin, subsequently sent a survey to alumni to ascertain interest in the idea. The survey was mailed to over 600 alumni drawn from the alumni records database, including those who have received a library science degree, who have a title or work address containing the word "library," or who indicated librarianship as their career code in alumni surveys.

Over 130 responses to the survey were received. They came from alumni who work in a wide variety of types of libraries and library positions. A large number of those responding voiced strong enthusiasm for the idea of the symposium. Respondents suggested numerous topics that they hoped would be included in the symposium, including the way in which Oberlin values have affected career choice and library work, the effects of digital technologies on

Two New Full-Text Databases in English Literature

The following new full-text databases from Chadwyck-Healey are now available to the Oberlin College community via the World Wide Web:

The English Poetry Database contains the texts of over 160,000 poems written in English by approximately 1,350 poets between the years 600 and 1900. It also includes the full text of over 4,400 poetry collections, many of them quite rare, listed in *The New Cambridge Bibliography of English Literature*.

English Verse Drama contains the full text of over 2,200 plays by more than 500 named authors and 300 anonymous works, from the Shrewsbury Fragments of the late thirteenth century through the end of the nineteenth century. EVD is based on materials listed in *The New Cambridge Bibliography of English Literature*, selecting materials that are written or intended for the stage and wholly or primarily in verse.

These databases join the six other Chadwyck-Healey databases made accessible by the Library earlier this year: *Editions and Adaptations of Shakespeare*, *English Prose Drama*, *Eighteenth Century Fiction*, *American Poetry Database*, *African-American Poetry Database*, and *The Bible in English* (see *Library Perspectives*, September 1997).

These databases are available to Oberlin Campus Network users through the Web version of OBIS at: http://obis.oberlin.edu (just search the database title).

Dissertations on the Web

The Oberlin College Library is now a subscriber to ProQuest Digital Dissertations, which provides online access to citations and abstracts for every title in the Dissertation Abstracts database.

With more than 1.4 million entries, UMI's Dissertation Abstracts database is the one central, authoritative source for information about doctoral dissertations and master's theses.

The database includes citations for materials ranging from the first U.S. dissertation, accepted in 1861, to those accepted as recently as last semester; those published from 1980 forward also include 350-word abstracts, written by the author. Citations for master's theses from 1988 forward include 150-word abstracts.

Of the 1.4 million titles listed, UMI offers over a million in full text.

The database represents the work of authors from over 1,000 North American graduate schools and European universities. Some 47,000 new dissertations and 12,000 new theses are added to the database each year.

To access ProQuest Digital Dissertations go the Library's Research Resources on the Internet Web page (http://www.oberlin.edu/~library/Schol_Res/), and click on "Databases & Indexes".

libraries, and the importance of keeping reading habits alive.

Raphael will coordinate the planning process by establishing a committee of those who expressed interest in helping to plan the symposium. An e-mail listserv is being set up at Oberlin to facilitate discussion among all those who volunteered.

An informal discussion will also be held in conjunction with a reception for Oberlin alumni librarians at the American Library Association annual conference in Washington, D.C. this summer.

Culpeper Foundation Preservation Grant Concludes

The Library has recently completed a multi-year project, funded by a $150,000 grant from the Charles E. Culpeper Foundation, to preserve collections endangered by acid paper deterioration (see *Library Perspectives*, February 1994).

The problem of paper deterioration is particularly challenging at Oberlin, since such a large portion of the Library's collections date from the late nineteenth and early twentieth centuries, when virtually all books and journals were produced on acidic paper. Acid weakens the cellulose fibers in paper, and over time leads to embrittled — and eventually unusable — materials. The useful life of acidic books, journals, and other print materials can be substantially extended through a process of deacidification, if the paper retains sufficient strength. Materials that have deteriorated to too great an extent remain useful only if they are "reformatted" — either by photocopying them to acid free paper and rebinding them or by converting them to microfilm, microfiche, or some other medium.

Under the Culpeper grant, the Library provided preservation treatment for over 7,200 endangered volumes that were considered most important for long-term retention. Over 6,400 volumes were selected for deacidification, including many monographs of more recent origin published in third world countries. Over 450 volumes were chosen for microformatting, including numerous titles related to Oberlin and Oberlin history. Over 300 volumes

continued page 7

Selected Materials Preserved under the Culpeper Grant

Special Collections materials:
* titles from the Violin Society of America/Goodkind Collection
* World War I pamphlets
* women's suffrage pamphlets
* rare maps of Yellowstone National Park
* Oberliniana:
    * brief biographies of prominent alumni, faculty, and staff
    * periodicals on Oberlin and the temperance movement
    * the *Oberlin News*
    * Oberlin College catalogs and official reports

Materials from the circulating collections:
* selections from art, classics, literature, science, poetry, and music
* titles published in East Asia, South Asia and Russia
* German language and music reference work
* monographs relating to travel and exploration in the New World
* books on Latin American history, politics, religion, and literature
* the complete musical scores of Brahms and Schubert

Purchases with Friends Funds...*from page 2*

phlets, Photographs, and Manuscripts, Primary Source Media). Contains primary materials from one of the most comprehensive research collections on Women's History, including diaries and other manuscripts, pamphlets, and photographs reproduced from the Schlesinger Library at Radcliffe, the Sophia Smith Collection at Smith College, and other depositories. The collection will support work by Professors Wendy Kozol and Carol Lasser.

2. *FBI Files*. Professor Albert Miller in the Religion Department teaches a course in the African American Religious Experience. Three microfilm collections documenting FBI investigations of the civil rights movement and of African American religious leaders will provide a rich selection of primary materials to support his courses. The three files are:

FBI File on Communist Infiltration of the Southern Christian Leadership Conference. Compiled 1958-1980 to "ascertain the degree of Communist party influence on the SCLC," the documents contained in the file highlight the attitude held by the FBI toward the SCLC and entire civil rights movement.

FBI File on Malcolm X. Documents Malcolm X's involvement with the Nation of Islam and on its behalf with the Socialist Workers Party and the Organization of African Unity.

FBI File on Elijah Muhammad. Documents Elijah Muhammed's leadership of the Nation of Islam and FBI view of him.

Facsimile for Special Collections ($2,316).

Der Musik-Codex Las Huelgas (Verlag Bibliotheca Rara). A facsimile autograph manuscript of a celebrated thirteenth-century musical work in the cloister of Santa Maria la Real de Las Huelgas in Madrid.

Library Perspectives, a newsletter for users and Friends of the Oberlin College Library, is issued two times a year. Printed from an endowed fund established by Benjamin A. and Emiko Custer. Editors: Ray English and Jessica Grim.

Cataloging Distinctions

The Oberlin College Library continues to be one of the nation's leading participants in cooperative cataloging endeavors. In the fall of 1995, the library earned "national-level Enhance status" as one of the earliest members of the Bibliographic Cooperative Program (BIBCO), the newest venture from the Library of Congress' Program for Cooperative Cataloging (PCC).

BIBCO libraries contribute bibliographic records, both full and core level, to national bibliographic utilities, such as OCLC. All headings in the BIBCO records follow standardized "authority control." These records are of the same high quality and equivalent authority as records from the Library of Congress. Approximately twenty libraries are currently participating in the program. The BIBCO project evolved from the National Coordinated Cataloging Program (NCCP), which became operational in 1988. In fiscal year 1997, program participants created nearly 30,000 program records.

While the Library of Congress will continue to administer this decentralized training program, most future training will be provided by regional trainers. John Sluk, Head of the Monographs

John Sluk

Department at Oberlin, was one of two trainers to travel to Vanderbilt University in December 1997. He and Joan Schuitema (Northwestern University) trained catalogers there in BIBCO record creation, and in the program's values of timely access and cost-effectiveness in cataloging.

Once again, a dedicated and knowledgeable staff enables us to participate in a nationally-recognized project which enriches not only the library catalog here at Oberlin, but the catalogs of thousands of other libraries throughout the world.

Dye Remarks
...from page 3

which the library increasingly employs new information technologies to extend access to library resources beyond our campus.

Oberlin's membership in OhioLINK is one of the developments that has greatly expanded access to library holdings outside of Oberlin. OhioLINK's more recent growth in full-text electronic resources appears equally promising. Then, too, we look toward the building of a new library: a critical part of the new science center that we envision is a new, expanded, and enhanced space for a comprehensive science library.

We are also working as librarians and faculty to continue to build on recent initiatives in information literacy. As I said to the Friends two years ago, the world of modern academic libraries is increasing our access to information at an incredible rate, but that world is also becoming more and more complicated. It is critically important that our students be well-grounded in the skills needed to use modern libraries if they are to take full advantage of the new and infinitely expanding world of instantly available information. Information literacy is essential not only for students' academic success here at Oberlin but also for life-long learning, a goal that remains fundamental to liberal education.

Again, I congratulate the Friends of the Library for the strong support you provide in Oberlin. And I look forward to hearing Professor Grafton's talk.

Lexis Nexis Now Available...*from page 1*

the legal literature is a full-time job these days. While Oberlin has a good collection of legal periodicals, we are not a law library and much is not available. Lexis-Nexis UNIVerse through the web is a godsend to both faculty teaching law-related subjects and students researching them."

Professor Walsh notes further that "Lexis-Nexis UNIVerse is also a terrific pedagogical tool. A student comes to my office with an idea and, instead of sending the

student off to the indices of legal periodicals, we can sit down at the terminal and explore. Nine times out of ten we hit the jackpot and an excited kid with a focus leaves the office. It is wonderful."

With Lexis-Nexis UNIVerse, Oberlin College students, faculty, and staff can access the full power of the Lexis-Nexis services in the now familiar environment of the World Wide Web. Lexis-Nexis UNIVerse can be accessed from within the Oberlin College com-

munity using direct URL (http://web.lexis-nexis.com/universe), or from the "Databases & Indexes" section of the Library's "Research Resources on the Internet" page (http://www.oberlin.edu/~library/Schol_Res/).

Information Literacy Workshops...*from page 1*

by the library staff provided an overview of information literacy concerns, demonstrated ways of accessing a variety of electronic information resources, and explored the development of effective assignments for increasing library research skills. Sessions taught by the OCTET staff covered a variety of topics related to classroom use of educational technologies, such as online syllabi, electronic conferencing, class listservs, and online papers and tests.

"I've been crowing all over the place about how wonderful the five faculty workshop sessions were!" said Katherine Jarjisian, Professor of Music Education. "I left each overwhelming and intense session completely energized and brimming about ways I could change this course or that. Of course, that's unrealistic, and I will have to change in painstakingly slow increments, but my students definitely will be doing more work (searching and discovering...) on-

Faculty at the Library/OCTET Workshop

line and developing skills to evaluate their electronic 'findings.' (So will I!!!)."

The second workshop offered by the Library was a half-day session designed specifically for faculty in the Politics Department. The workshop was taught primarily by the Main Library Reference Department staff and focused to a large extent on electronic resources useful for study and research in

Politics. It was followed by a wide-ranging discussion of how the Library and the Politics Department might work more productively to develop information literacy skills in students who major in Politics.

The Library hopes to conduct additional workshops for individual departments in order to further explore information literacy issues with faculty at the disciplinary level.

Culpeper Foundation...*from page 5*

were reformatted through preservation photocopying, including reference works and individual monographs.

The Culpeper grant enabled the Library to develop new preservation processing workflows and to define preservation selection criteria based on subject matter, condition, and use. The process of selecting items for preservation also provided an opportunity to

purchase numerous replacement volumes that were still available from commercial publishers.

The Library is especially pleased that the Culpeper Foundation grant served as a catalyst for creating a new preservation endowment, income from which will be used to fund similar collection preservation activities on an ongoing basis. The endowment, which now stands at approximately

$160,000, was built through alumni contributions, including a major gift from William G. Roe of the Class of 1964. The Library hopes to continue building the endowment in the future.

The Library wishes to express its sincere appreciation and gratitude to the Culpeper Foundation for supporting this significant expansion of its collection preservation efforts.

Grafton Talk Available...*from page 3*

ferences between reading then, and now—the need to learn Latin, the difficulty of obtaining books at all, and the use of "professional readers" who were employed to help prepare young men to go off into the world. Referring to the slides of magnificent examples of Renais-

sance books, he noted that "What you have here is reading taken seriously in a way that I don't think we take the use of texts very often anymore."

Copies of the video tape of Professor Grafton's talk are available for $6 (includes shipping and han-

dling) from: Friends of the Library, Mudd Center, Oberlin College, Oberlin OH 44074.

Please do not send payment with your request. You will be billed when the videotape is shipped. Allow four weeks for delivery.

JOIN US. BE A FRIEND.

The **Friends of the Oberlin College Library** provide significant support for special acquisitions and programs that help the library fulfill its fundamental role in the academic life of the college.

Members receive the *Library Perspectives* newsletter (published two times a year), invitations to Friends programs, and other privileges. Most of all, Friends have the satisfaction of supporting Oberlin's outstanding library.

Annual membership categories: ☐ $1 Student
☐ $25 Friend   ☐ $100 Sponsor
☐ $30 Couple   ☐ $500 Patron
☐ $50 Associate   ☐ $1000 Benefactor
Please return this coupon with your membership contribution to:

Friends of the Oberlin College Library
Mudd Center, Oberlin, OH 44074

Name: _____

Street: _____

City: _____

State: _____ Zip Code: _____

Please make checks payable to Oberlin College.
Friends contributions are tax deductible.

Printed on recycled paper

Library Perspectives
Oberlin College Library
Mudd Center
148 West College Street
Oberlin, OH 44074

Non-profit
Organization
U.S. Postage
PAID
Oberlin, Ohio
Permit No. 8

Friends of the Library Newsletter
Wellesley College

Volume 14, number 1   *Spring 1998*

FRIENDS VOTE TO FUND NEW CONSERVATION FACILITY
by Jane Hedberg, Serials Librarian and Preservation Administrator

On November 19, 1997, the Friends of the Library Steering Committee voted to contribute $250,000 toward construction of a new Conservation Facility. This extraordinary gift, added to endowment fund income already committed by Micheline Jedrey, Librarian of the College, completed our fundraising efforts in one dramatic gesture. I cannot adequately convey how much this gift means to Preservation Department staff and students or how grateful we are to all of the Friends for their unprecedented support. We have long dreamed of a new Conservation Facility and to say we are thrilled would be an understatement.

Since 1975, the present Conservation Lab has been located in Technical Services on the main floor of Clapp Library. We perform a reasonably full range of conservation treatments: paper mending, book spine repair, book cover replacement, box making, pamphlet binding, and all the ancillary functions supporting those activities. Although we are glad to work in close proximity to our Library colleagues, this location has three major drawbacks. First, as we have expanded our conservation efforts, we have crowded more and more equipment into too small an area and increasingly encroached on others' space. Second, sharing "office" space limits our execution of treatments. The student workers who affix metal grommets to classroom maps must do the necessary hammering in a remote area of the Library because the noise is disturbing to other staff. Washing paper is impossible because the large washing trays are unwieldy and too messy. Third, built-in shelves, cupboards, and book stacks hamper our ability to reorganize Lab space.

Our new Conservation Facility will be designed to minimize limitations and expand possibilities. It will be located next to the Book Arts Lab on the fourth floor of Clapp Library in a large, high-ceilinged, naturally lit room. Present plans call for seven custom-made workbenches, with a press or paper cutter beside each, clustered around the large pieces of equipment which must be shared. Most benches will be outfitted with the appropriate tools and supplies for a particular type of treatment, with one bench dedicated solely to creating enclosures for

Conservation Facility continued on page 3.

This is for me?

It is, if you are a current Friend of the Library OR a 1997 Wellesley graduate. If you're a recent alum, we hope you will become excited by the Friends' work described here and that you will join us.

Annual membership is $15 (for those out of college five years or less) or $35 for others. Checks, made payable to Wellesley College, should be sent to Friends of the Library, Wellesley College, Margaret Clapp Library, Wellesley MA 02181-8239.

Help Wellesley's most treasured resource, the center of its life, continue and grow!

NOTED THERAPISTS DISCUSS WOMEN AND RELATIONSHIPS APRIL 15

In a society that often demeans empathy as a "female" trait, psychological theorists Jean Baker Miller and Irene Pierce Stiver see women's ability to make and maintain relationships as a new model for the psychological development of all. On Wednesday, April 15, at 4:45 p.m. in the Clapp Library Lecture Room, Miller and Stiver will discuss *The Healing Connection: How Women Form Relationships in Therapy and in Life*, their new book applying Miller's

Jean Baker Miller

groundbreaking theory of relational psychology to patients in their practices.

The dominant psychodynamic model of the twentieth century states that healthy adulthood requires separation and autonomy. Relational psychology, on the other hand, defines mental health in terms of connection-in particular, of empathetic listening and responding. Mutually empathetic interactions mutually empower and foster growth.

Noted Therapists continued on page 3.

MAKING MEMORIES: CREATING AN ARTIST'S BOOK FROM PERSONAL EXPERIENCE
by Jill Triplett Bent, Special Collections Assistant

During the spring of 1997, Marilyn Hatch, my co-worker in Special Collections, attended a calligraphy workshop at New Mexico's Ghost Ranch. Her cross-country train trip and Ghost Ranch experiences prompted her to create a personal journal, the record of her trip in pictures and words. Drawing on her artistic abilities, Marilyn used hand-made paste paper, calligraphy, found objects, color photocopies, sketches, and watercolors to create a unique book capturing her own experience and the feel of the southwest.

After seeing Marilyn's book, I felt inspired to make one myself. I knew just the subject. Over the summer to come, my husband and I planned a honeymoon in Turkey. Would Marilyn consider giving a workshop the following winter on creating a personal journal? She was enthusiastic about the project. Ruth Rogers, Special Collections Librarian, wholeheartedly supported the idea. Although initially limited to twelve, the course attracted almost twenty. Our final count was fourteen.

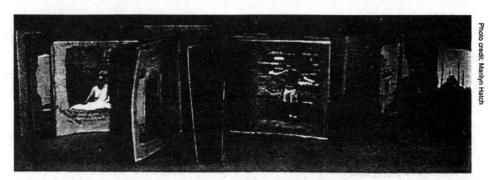

Photo credit: Marilyn Hatch

For the first class, Marilyn selected examples of artists' books from Special Collections. Book artist Alisa Golden's *Nina, Rose and Me*, a tribute to her sister, included xeroxes of old family pictures on colored paper and printed reflections about childhood. We looked at Marilyn Hatch's book *Carolyn*, a response to Golden's book and tribute to Marilyn's own sister. Illustrated with hand-colored photocopies, it formed a tunnel when opened. We were inspired by the work of other sisters: Dorothy and Susan Yule's *Souvenirs of Great Cities* contained four tiny books folded into an accordion format displaying the Eiffel Tower, Golden Gate Bridge, and Tower of London in color pop-up sketches. Alicia McKim's *Home on the Range* opened to reveal six panoramas of western ranching scenes, with multiple folding layers of scenery forming the shape of a star. Marilyn then gave in-depth presentations of techniques embodied in these books: a simple pamphlet stitch, an accordion fold, an etching press, a photocopy transfer. In addition, she encouraged us to develop our own techniques.

During the second class, we created paste papers with a mixture of acrylics and flour and water paste on damp paper. These would eventually form the pages of our journals. My goal was to evoke the landscape and culture of Turkey. I chose strong colors: bold blues to represent the sea and sky, rich yellows to capture the stucco façades of buildings and heat of the sun, a deep coral tinged with red and gold to suggest the ambiance of the Egyptian Spice Market and color of walls beneath climbing roses and rosemary plants on the breakfast terrace of our hotel. I used blue-black sprinkled with gold to represent Istanbul's sparkling lights reflected in the waters of the Bosphorus Sea. Around the room, my classmates created colorful patterns-some subtle and soft, some bold, others downright funky. Throughout, Marilyn made herself available to all fourteen of us whenever we needed her help or advice.

By class three, most of us were well underway. I knew I wanted to include photos and descriptions of the major sites we had visited: the Topkapi Palace, the Aya Sofya, the Blue Mosque, and the ruins of Ephesus. I also wanted to include details: the wonderful Turkish food, the rooftop garden at our hotel, the bike ride we took on the island of Büyükada, the markets and rug merchants, and our interactions with the Turkish people. I made drawings painted over with watercolor of our daily breakfast at the Empress Zoe Hotel, the Turkish pastries and other delights from the Spice Market, pottery and rug patterns that captured my imagination, a sarcophagus from the museum in Ephesus, an old house in Selçuk, the benches and umbrellas on the beaches of the Aegean coast, and women in traditional dress.

Making Memories continued on page 4.

2

Unique Cards

From The

Wellesley College Library Collections
Proceeds to Benefit the Friends of the Wellesley College Library

1. Postcards of photographs (1880 - 1915) from the Library's archives
    in black and white.
    Set of 16 cards (2 each of 8 images)....................................$10.00

2. Color illustrated note cards of winter scenes from *A Day on
    Skates: The Story of a Dutch Picnic*, by Hilda van Stockum, 1934,
    Special Collections. (Blank inside)
    Box of 8 cards (2 each of 4 images) with envelopes..............$10.00

3. Color floral note cards from *Botanical Garden*, Benjamin Maund,
    London (1825-26). (Blank inside)
    Box of 8 cards (2 of each design) with envelopes..................$10.00

ORDER FORM

Detach and Enclose with your Check

1. Postcards   _____ sets @ $10.00 per set $_____

2. Winter Scenes _____ boxes @ $10.00 per box $_____

3. Floral Notes   _____ boxes @ $10.00 per box $_____

    Add $2.00 shipping and handling per box/set $_____
    Over 5 boxes - $1.50 per box shipping and handling
                                              TOTAL $_____

Please Make Checks Payable to: Wellesley College Library

Mail To: Librarian's Office
                Clapp Library
                Wellesley College
                106 Central Street
                Wellesley, MA 02181-8239

Margaret Clapp Library

Conservation Facility continued from page 1.
Special Collections materials. There will be a large washing sink for cleaning or deacidifying paper, a fume hood for safe use of alcohol or other chemicals, and a walk-in storage closet so our supplies of board are always nearby. Sue Leong, our collections conservator, will have an office, and the Library's subject selectors will have an area where they can review preservation decisions. Whenever possible, the furniture and equipment will be moveable so the space can change as required. With access controlled by a digital one-card system and fire suppression supplied by a sophisticated sprinkler system, the area will be secure.

As a first draft of our dream, the Library's architect, Shepley, Bulfinch, Richardson and Abbott have completed some very exciting schematic drawings. Since Shepley is just finishing a similar facility at Harvard University, we anticipate learning a great deal from their recent experience. When we are finished, we plan to have the best facility of its kind in New England.

Since 1984, the Friends of the Library have generously supported our conservation efforts by giving us equipment, furniture, and funds for supplies. Our board shear (named Bob by the students for its strength and solidity), large bronze press (named Big Ben for its size), table-model creaser (not yet named), plus flat-file and board storage units were all gifts from you. Preservation Department staff have always appreciated these gifts for the way they have both improved our work and represented Friends' interest. This donation to the new Conservation Facility culminates more than a decade of generosity and dedication to preserving the book at Wellesley College. Thank you.

Noted Therapists continued from page 1.
Disconnection-failure of empathy in relationships-causes psychological problems. In *The Healing Connection*, Miller and Stiver show how three kinds of disconnection in childhood-an unexpressed but haunting family secret, an emotionally inaccessible parent, or a child forced by circumstances to function as a parent-lead to a disinclination in adulthood to form intimate relationships. Unlike Freudian psychotherapy, in relational psychotherapy an active, sympathetic therapist participates with her patient in dialogue that changes both.

Photo credit: William Mercer

Irene Pierce Stiver

An alumna of Sarah Lawrence College, Jean Baker Miller received her M.D. from Columbia University. Author of the landmark text *Toward a New Psychology of Women*, she is a practicing psychiatrist and psychoanalyst, clinical professor of psychiatry at the Boston University School of Medicine, and founding director of the Jean Baker Miller Training Institute at the Stone Center, Wellesley Centers for Women. Irene Pierce Stiver was graduated from Brooklyn College and received an M.A. and Ph.D. from Cornell University. Author of over twenty-five articles and chapters, many as part of the Stone Center's *Work in Progress* series, she is Director Emerita of the Psychology Department at McLean Hospital, Lecturer in Psychology at Harvard Medical School, and a Founding Scholar of the Jean Baker Miller Training Institute.

CALENDAR

APRIL 7
Steering Committee meeting, Friends of the Library. Sanger Room, 3-4:30 p.m.

APRIL 15
Jean Baker Miller and Irene Pierce Stiver discuss *The Healing Connection*. Sponsored by Friends of the Library and the Stone Center, Wellesley Centers for Women. Library Lecture Room, 4:45-5:45 p.m. Refreshments, 4:15 p.m.

APRIL 22
Spring *Authors on Stage* program. Sponsored by Wellesley College Alumnae of Boston. The following authors will discuss their work: Douglass Shand-Tucci, *The Art of Scandal*; Anita Shreve, *The Pilot's Wife*; and Martha Cooley, *The Archivist*. Wellesley College Club. Coffee, 9:45 a.m. Program, 10:30 a.m.

REUNION, JUNE 6
Tours of new Knapp Media and Technology Center, Special Collections, and Research Resources Department. 11 a.m. and 2 p.m. Sponsored by Friends of the Library. Meet at Knapp Center entrance, Clapp Library.

EXHIBITIONS

NOW THROUGH MAY 15
Legendary Lovers: Books and Manuscripts from the 15th-20th Centuries. Daphnis and Chloe, Petrarch and Laura, Robert and Elizabeth Browning, and others.

MAY 28-AUGUST 14
The Consequences of War: Poetry, Graphic Art, and Documents from Special Collections.

Clapp Library, 4th floor, Special Collections.

3

Making Memories continued from page 2.

At our fourth class, I began tearing my paste papers down to the size I wanted and affixing color photocopies, along with my watercolors and sketches, to each page. At this point, I realized that completing my book by the sixth class was going to require overtime. Before going home at night, I spent half an hour in the Book Arts Lab. I was not alone: everyone else in my class was as engrossed in her project as I, so the Lab was a center of after-hours activity.

During the fifth class, I wrote my text in by hand. Marilyn then demonstrated binding techniques so that during the sixth and final class we could make our own hardcover bindings. Binding requires dexterity, not my strong suit, but as I put my newly bound book into the book press, I felt proud of my final product. I was amazed to see what we had accomplished: the range of creativity and level of craftsmanship were remarkable. After working with books for five years, I had finally made one of my own.

For a private viewing of the books made in this class, please visit us on the World Wide Web at http://www.wellesley.edu//Library/Wintex/Journal_as_artist's_book.html.

YOLEN DELIGHTS LOCAL SCHOOLCHILDREN

After discussing her new book, *Child of Faerie, Child of Earth*, as part of last November's *Authors on Stage*, Jane Yolen met with Irene Gruenfeld's fourth-grade class from Wellesley's Bates School. The class later wrote to Gina Wickwire CE '81, who had arranged the gathering.

Dear Mrs Wickwire,

Thank you for arranging our visit with Jane Yolen. We know you were very busy that day and we appreciate that you took the time to let us meet her. We had a great time talking with Jane Yolen. There are so many things we learned, we can't fit them all on one page. One of the funniest things she said was that she wanted to be a ballerina until she discovered chocolate chip cookies. One interesting thing we found out is that Jane Yolen can't do any more *Piggins* books because the illustrator, Jane Dyer, won't illustrate any more *Piggins* books unless it is *Piggins on the Titanic*. If you were a kid and you were studying about Jane Yolen, you would understand how lucky we felt. It was very generous of you to let us come in and meet Jane Yolen. Thank you again.

4-Gruenfeld

Thanks to Betty Febo, Publicity Assistant, for *Newsletter* design.

Wellesley College
Friends of the Library
Margaret Clapp Library
106 Central Street
Wellesley, MA 02181-8239

Publications

Charles E. Shain Library
Connecticut College
270 Mohegan Ave.
New London, CT 06320-4196

Julia Rogers Library
Goucher College
1021 Dulaney Valley Rd.
Baltimore, MD 21204

Smith College Libraries
Smith College
Northampton, MA 01063

Oberlin College Library
Oberlin College
Oberlin, OH 44074

Plant House at Connecticut College

A Wood-Engraving

by

JOHN DE POL, A.N.A.

Plant House: A Wood Engraving by John De Pol

Plant House is one of three residential buildings erected in the first years of Connecticut College. It was named for Morton F. Plant, a summer resident of the area who took a practical interest in the new College, contributed generously to it, and served as the first chairman of its Board of Trustees.

In May, 1913, two years after the grant of the College charter, Morton Plant gave the money to construct two residences near New London Hall, the first College building. These were built in 1914 in the late Gothic style of Tudor England and named Plant House and Branford House. They were soon joined by a third, Blackstone House, to form a quadrangle. The intent of the College's founders was to associate the idea of the American college with the English universities at Oxford and Cambridge by using the architectural style historically linked to the notion of a learned community.

Of the three residential buildings, Plant House is the more completely realized as a domestic building of Tudor times. Its mullioned casement windows and arched oak doors suggest the late medieval house. The area around the main entrance was given especially prominent features, as with the porch above which projects an oriel window appropriate to an Elizabethan manor house, or the small tower at the angle which gives the impression of a castle stairtower but was in fact to contain the telephone.

Plant House and its neighbors were designed by the New York firm of Ewing and Chappell. George S. Chappell was a New Londoner trained in Paris. The architects and the College officers believed that "the buildings will require practically no ornament, gaining their beauty from the simple masses of the architectural forms themselves..." (Preliminary Announcement of Connecticut College, 1914, quoted in Gertrude E. Noyes, A History of Connecticut College, 1982).

* * *

John De Pol must be numbered among the greatest living American wood engravers. After his retirement in 1978 as an art consultant in the financial printing industry, what had been a subsidiary but serious interest became a wholly absorbing occupation. His output of illustrations for Yellow Barn Press books and those of the Pickering Press, the Red Ozier Press and the Stone House Press has been prodigious and his artistry and skill have been honored wherever fine printing is appreciated. His prints are to be found in the collections of museums, universities, and libraries, including the Charles E. Shain Library at Connecticut College.

In the course of an exhibition of John De Pol's work in the Charles E. Shain Library, Mr. De Pol visited the campus from time to time and on one of those visits offered to produce an engraved wood block for the benefit of the College and its library. A number of subjects were suggested and from these John De Pol chose to depict the part of Plant House that so completely corresponds to an almost universal notion of what constitutes the ideal college, with its implications of a settled community of antique foundation separated by time and granite walls from the work-a-day world.

Charles Price
Professor Emeritus of Art History
Connecticut College

Wood block illustrations and moveable type have been used together since the beginnings of printing. There have been times when the use of the wood block for book illustration has receded from favor, but the twentieth century has seen an enthusiastic revival of wood engraving, especially among owners of private presses and collectors of fine books.

Wood engraving lends itself to small-scale work; indeed, it is virtually limited to it by the nature of the medium. The engraving is done with sharp-pointed tools known as burins. The burin cuts a line in the surface of an end-grain block - a block that has been cut across the grain. The completed block is surface-inked and the image is transferred to a sheet of paper with a press.

Plant House was drawn and engraved on a maple block and is here printed for the first time by permission of the artist.

Published in an edition of 165 copies
by
The Friends of the Connecticut College Library
1993

Charles E. Shain Library
Greer Music Library

New London, Connecticut 06320

Engraving: Created by artist John De Pol for Connecticut College on the occasion of an exhibition of his work in the library, the engraving is signed by the artist and presented on heavyweight cream-colored paper in a flocked gray folder. The engraving is suitable for framing. Copies were both distributed and made available for sale.

"WITHIN THE LINES"

A Guide to the
Passano Collection
on
Women of the South
During the
Civil War

The Goucher College Library
Baltimore, Maryland
October 1995

Edith Wharton card: 6 ¾″ x 5 ½″ on cream paper
with green image and black type.

"Wharton became known to all her friends as a super-gardener. Madame Saint-René Taillandier, who translated Wharton's fiction in her last years, used the garden as a metaphor for their friendship: 'We met, so to put it, in a garden of the mind, among the choice roses of her growing, the homelier violets of mine; and there we talked at large of other 'garden fancies,' curious and far-fetched, the works of our literary friends. My image is at any rate one that well beseems her. Which of us all who knew her, however slightly, can recall her name without the vision of a garden, perfect in its beauty?'"

****

Wharton described the garden at the Mount, her home in Lenox, Massachusetts, in a letter to W. Morton Fullerton, dated July 3, 1911: "The heat is bad, and so is the drought; but in spite of both the place is really beautiful, and so much leafier & more 'fondu' than two years ago that I was amazed at the success of my [efforts]. Decidedly, I'm a better landscape gardener than novelist, and this place, every line of which is my own work, far surpasses the House of Mirth."

Excerpts from Eleanor Dwight, *Edith Wharton: An Extraordinary Life* (New York: Harry N. Abrams, Inc., 1994); reprinted with permission of the publisher. Illustration reproduced from the binding of Reginald Blomfield and F. Inigo Thomas, *The Formal Garden in England* (London: Macmillan & Co., 1892). The Smith College Libraries copy in the Mortimer Rare Book Room is from the Library of Beatrix Jones Farrand, Edith Wharton's niece.

Two hundred and fifty copies printed on the occasion of the Friends of the Smith College Libraries Annual Lecture, presented by Eleanor Dwight, entitled "Edith Wharton: An Extraordinary Gardener," April 7, 1995, Northampton, Massachusetts. Typographic design by Barbara B. Blumenthal. Printing by Pioneer Valley Printing Company, Easthampton, Massachusetts.

FRIENDS OF THE OBERLIN COLLEGE LIBRARY

NANCY SCHROM DYE

❧

READING AND THE FUTURE OF LIBRARIES

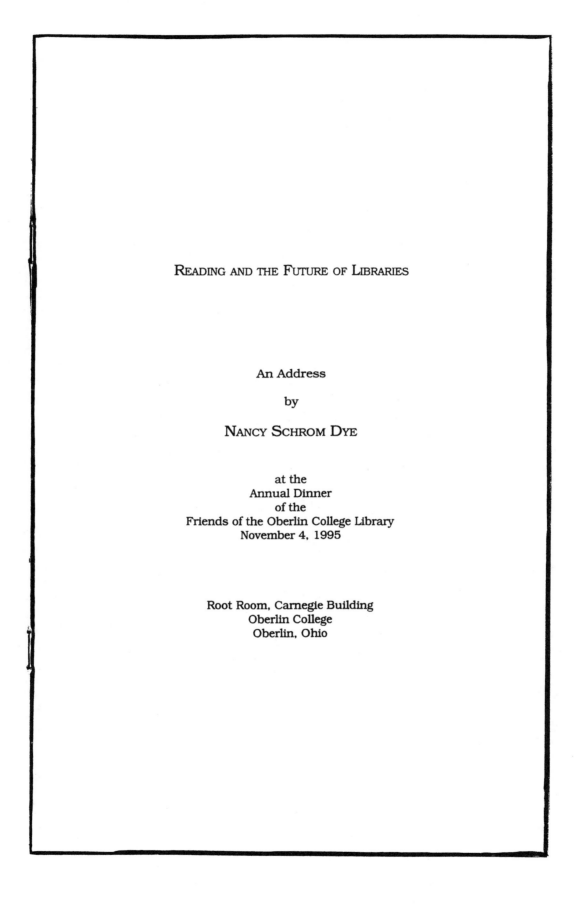

READING AND THE FUTURE OF LIBRARIES

An Address

by

NANCY SCHROM DYE

at the
Annual Dinner
of the
Friends of the Oberlin College Library
November 4, 1995

Root Room, Carnegie Building
Oberlin College
Oberlin, Ohio

Miscellaneous

Ralph M. Besse Library
Ursuline College
2550 Lander Road
Cleveland, OH 44124-4398

Houston Cole Library
Jacksonville State University
North Pelham Rd.
Jacksonville, AL 36265

L.A. Beeghly Library
Ohio Wesleyan University
43 University Ave.
Delaware, OH 43015

Notecard: 4″ x 5″ on cream paper
with brown-tone image.

Friends of Houston Cole Library

_____

Is A Member In Good Standing

Through Calendar Year_____

_____ Secretary

Bookplate (above): gray card stock
with red lettering.
Membership card (below): white card stock
with red lettering.

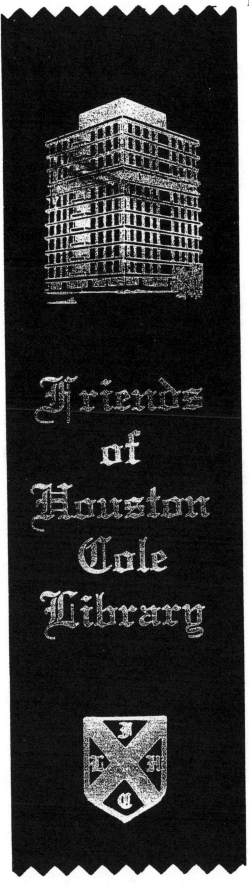

Bookmark: Burgundy satin with silver print.

Houston Cole Library

Notecard: 4″ x 5½″ on white card stock
with black image.

Friends of the Ohio Wesleyan Libraries

Christmas card: Inside message "Season's Greetings and Best Wishes for a Happy New Year."